P·E·A·R·L·S

FREAKS *the* #*%# OUT

Other *Pearls Before Swine* Collections

Because Sometimes You Just Gotta Draw a Cover with Your Left Hand

Larry in Wonderland

When Pigs Fly

50,000,000 Pearls Fans Can't Be Wrong

The Saturday Evening Pearls

Macho Macho Animals

The Sopratos

Da Brudderhood of Zeeba Zeeba Eata

The Ratvolution Will Not Be Televised

Nighthogs

This Little Piggy Stayed Home

BLTs Taste So Darn Good

Treasuries

Pearls Blows Up

Pearls Sells Out

The Crass Menagerie

Lions and Tigers and Crocs, Oh My!

Sgt. Piggy's Lonely Hearts Club Comic

Gift Book

Da Crockydile Book o' Frendsheep

P·E·A·R·L·S
FREAKS the #*%# OUT

★ A (FREAKY) PEARLS BEFORE SWINE TREASURY ★

BY STEPHAN PASTIS

Andrews McMeel
Publishing®

Kansas City · Sydney · London

Andrews McMeel Publishing, LLC
an Andrews McMeel Universal company
1130 Walnut Street, Kansas City, Missouri 64106

www.andrewsmcmeel.com

15 16 17 18 SDB 10 9 8 7 6 5 4

ISBN: 978-1-4494-2302-5

Library of Congress Control Number: 2012935818

Pearls Before Swine can be viewed on the Internet at
www.pearlscomic.com

These strips appeared in newspapers from August 23, 2009, to February 27, 2011.

——— **ATTENTION: SCHOOLS AND BUSINESSES** ———

Andrews McMeel books are available at quantity discounts with bulk purchase for educational, business, or sales promotional use. For information, please e-mail the Andrews McMeel Publishing Special Sales Department:
specialsales@amuniversal.com

Dedication

To my ever-vigilant editor, Reed Jackson, the thin red line of protection between me and the vulnerable masses, and the only guy I know who ever censored the word "banana."

Introduction

Cartoonists are shut-ins.

They don't leave home. And with good reason.

They can't control what happens out there.

So they stay inside. And create a world of their own. A world they can control.

The reclusiveness doesn't start when they become syndicated. That's just when they start getting paid for it.

The reclusiveness starts when they're young.

And I was no exception.

I spent most of my childhood in my room. Mostly drawing. But also playing with my *Star Wars* figurines.

I didn't have many friends. And those who were my friends were my cousins. So they didn't have a choice.

I didn't go to the high school football games. I didn't go to parties. And I didn't go to dances.

Except one.

A dance in my senior year of high school.

I can't tell you why I decided to leave my hermit shell that day. Maybe I felt obligated. Maybe I started liking girls. Maybe I just got bored of playing with *Star Wars* dolls.

But the girl I asked to go to the dance was named Julie. We were in all the same classes. She was very smart and kind, and I thought if I asked her, she wouldn't laugh and point.

As it turned out, she did laugh and point. But she still said yes. And gave me her address.

As I drove up to her house that night, I realized that her family had a whole lot of money. The house was a huge, multimillion-dollar mansion fronted by a football field–size yard and a tall, ornate gate.

All of which made me feel very small as I puttered up the long circular driveway in my mom's Pontiac Phoenix, a car that had a tendency to stall out when making right turns.

Fortunately, Julie's driveway curved to the left.

I walked up to the large double doors and rang the doorbell. It played Bach's Fugue in D Minor.

There, inside the princely foyer, was the entire family. Julie, her younger brother, her mom, her dad.

I sat down with them in their ornate living room, right next to a lamp that was worth more than my entire house.

I found out that night that Julie's dad was the vice president of a prominent Fortune 500 company. Hence, all the money.

The conversation that followed was awkward and obligatory.

Awkward because all conversations with me are awkward.

Obligatory because when you pick up a man's daughter for a high school dance, you apparently have to do more than honk the horn and wave.

So we sat and talked about the only mundane topics we could think up to fill the time.

The dance, our classes, future college plans.

And oh yes, guns.

I'm not quite sure how that abrupt transition was achieved. ("College is very important. Do you like guns?")

But Julie's dad had one he wanted to show me.

He was so soft-spoken and corporate that I didn't take this as the act of an overprotective father. He just seemed proud of his gun.

So he went to the closet and pulled out this very long, sleek, rifle-looking thing.

He called it an "elephant gun." And it must have been good at what it did because I didn't see any elephants.

The whole thing was an odd scene.

This short, rather meek man holding a gun that was two inches longer than himself, while his wife and the rest of us watched from overstuffed Louis XIV chairs.

But there we were. An already awkward group of people made more so by the fact that one of us was now armed.

"Take a look at it," he said as he walked over and held it out in front of me.

"Nice," I said, not knowing how to compliment a gun, an elephant, or any combination of the two.

"It's designed so you can't really miss," he said, pressing the butt of the gun against his shoulder and looking down the barrel.

I looked over at Julie. I gave her my best "We really should be going" expression. She replied with her best "He's my dad. What am I supposed to do?" expression.

So I turned back to look at her dad.

And that's when I heard it.

The concussive boom.

For two feet from my head, the gun had gone off.

And fortunately for my head, not in its direction.

But toward the foyer.

A foyer that was now destroyed.

The fancy double doors, the Persian rug, the hardwood floor. All filled with holes.

Her dad stared dumbfounded at the gun.

"I didn't think it was loaded," he said faintly.

It was so trite. So cliché.

I, for one, was hoping for something more noble. Something like, "Did you see that charging elephant?"

But no. He was too in shock.

Too disturbed.

The predictable chaos ensued.

The screaming mom. The excited son. The mortified Julie.

And clinging to the curtains at the back of the living room, as far from the decimated foyer as could be. . . .

. . . the trembling cartoonist.

Determined to never leave the safety of his *Star Wars* dolls again.

—Stephan Pastis
September 2013

I really don't have anything to say about this strip, but I feel bad allowing the first strip in the book to pass without comment. So there. I've said something.

Don't most pirates only have *one* hook? Perhaps I was too lazy to draw hands.

If I had really been thinking, I would have run at least one of these on "Talk Like A Pirate" day (September 19). But I wasn't.

My family and I were recently at the ranch of *Zits* cartoonist Jerry Scott. While walking through the hills, we found the skull of a cow. It still had some bloodstains on it. We were so excited we took it home. That's the kind of family I have.

This strip is bad. Perhaps I should give refunds for the portion of the book it occupies.

WHAT ARE YOU DOING, RAT?

I HAVE DECIDED TO BECOME AN ASCETIC MONK. I RENOUNCE ALL THE TRAPPINGS OF THIS WORLDLY LIFE. I SHALL HENCEFORTH LIVE IN THE FOREST.

HOW ARE YOU GONNA EAT?

I SHALL EAT WHAT THE FOREST PROVIDES. I THINK I'VE SEEN ENOUGH 'MAN VS. WILD' ON 'DISCOVERY' TO MAKE THAT POSSIBLE.

BUT YOU'LL STARVE.

NO. FOR IF IT COMES RIGHT DOWN TO IT, I SHALL CALL THE PIZZA DELIVERY GUY.

YOU CAN'T ORDER A PIZZA.

I CAN WITH MY 'iPhone'!

YOU CAN'T BRING AN 'iPhone'!

OH, AND I SUPPOSE YOU'RE GONNA SAY I CAN'T BRING MY 'Xbox' OR THIS KEG OF BEER EITHER.

YOU CAN'T!

THEN HOW WILL I ENTERTAIN MY DALLAS COWBOY CHEERLEADER?

I GIVE UP.

YOUR FRIEND IS QUITE A BUZZ-KILLER.

YES. WE SHALL PRAY FOR HIM.

I really do watch a ton of *Man vs. Wild*. And every time I watch an episode, I'm convinced that Bear Grylls has pushed it too far and is finally going to die. Yet somehow he doesn't. The guy is the closest thing we have to a superhero.

There is one type of these packing peanuts that dissolves in water. When I find some in a package, I'll spend hours making each one of them disappear in the bathroom sink. I figure it's the closest I'll ever come to being a magician.

I do not know the *Love Is* cartoonists. But I know that their comic is supposed to be uplifting. That's the opposite of *Pearls*. I try to bring people *down*.

BAD NEWS. ONE OF YOUR CROCS GOT SHIPPED TO THE 'LOVE IS' COMIC STRIP AND ATE THE NAKED GUY. NOW THE NAKED GIRL IS A WIDOW AND THE STRIP'S BEEN RE-TITLED 'LOVE ISN'T.'

OHMYGAWD! WHAT DID THE NAKED GIRL DO ABOUT THE CROC?

WELL, TURNS OUT SHE WAS ONE HEAT-PACKING MAMA. AND NOW SHE'S GOT A PACKAGE FOR YOU.

'LOVE IS... DOING YOUR OWN TAXIDERMY.'

MIND IF I HANG IT IN MY STUDY?

Maybe *Love Isn't* should be my next comic strip. It could run right next to *Love Is*. But instead of having two naked people in love, I'll show two clothed people fighting.

WHOA. DO YOU THINK WE COULD FAST-FORWARD THROUGH THIS PART OF OUR D.V.D.?

WHAT ARE YOU TALKING ABOUT? IT'S JUST THE F.B.I.'s ANTI-PIRACY WARNING.

PLEASE DON'T INVITE YOUR PIRATE FRIEND TO OUR HOUSE.

HERE. HAVE A TISSUE.

I AM POPULAR. WOULD YOU LIKE TO KNOW *WHY* I AM POPULAR?

NO.

I HAVE STARTED A 'FACEBOOK' PAGE UNDER THE NAME 'PEARLS RAT' AND I CURRENTLY HAVE 475 FRIENDS.

SORRY, RAT, BUT I HAVE A 'FACEBOOK' PAGE TOO AND I'M A LITTLE TOO MATURE TO BELIEVE THE NUMBER OF FRIENDS YOU HAVE ON AN INTERNET SOCIAL NETWORK DETERMINES YOUR POPULARITY.

YOUR MOUTH SAYS 'MATURE,' BUT YOUR FACEBOOK FRIEND COUNT SCREAMS 'LOSER.'

CHECK, PLEASE.

Sadly, I really do keep track of the number of people on my *Pearls* fan page. To find it, just search for "Author Stephan Pastis" on Facebook. The profile pic is my drawing of myself. Go there and click the "like" button so I can fulfill my lifelong goal of catching Ashton Kutcher. (Current count: Stephan—23,300 fans Ashton—10,784,217)

15

This really did happen to the first Rat page I created. I think Facebook has since changed its policy about fictional characters.

I really liked this ballerina character, but I think I was the only one. I'm not sure why, but she just did not catch on.

I forgot to add the dot-shading to her hair in the second panel. Maybe that's why she didn't catch on.

HEY, ZEBRA, I THINK I JUST HEARD A NOISE FROM UNDER YOUR FLOOR. / **IT'S THE CROCS. THEY'VE DISCOVERED THE CRAWL SPACE. THEY'RE TRYING TO USE IT TO GET INTO THE HOUSE.**

HOW DO YOU KNOW IT'S THEM? / **BECAUSE EVERY TIME THEY SMASH THEIR SNOUTS ON THE FLOOR JOISTS, THEY TRY TO DISGUISE WHO THEY ARE.** / **THUD**

Whoa. Me is one huge ant.

OH. / Hey...My snout really hurt, Floyd. / Shut mouf, Bob. We is ants.

When we lived in Albany, California, I used to draw the strip in our basement. There was a small door that led from the basement to the crawlspace under the house. I always used to hear noises coming from the other side of that door. When we moved out, the house inspector revealed that there was an entire family of raccoons living in that crawlspace. And here I thought it was my wife, Staci, who was tipping over the garbage cans every night.

HEY, GOAT...COME ON IN. I JUST FINISHED SETTING UP OUR NEW CAT SCRATCHING POST. / **I DIDN'T KNOW YOU GOT A CAT.**

WE DIDN'T. / **THEN WHY'D YOU GET A CAT SCRATCHING POST?**

ROWR / **SO OUR FERAL BALLERINA WOULD STOP DESTROYING THE FURNITURE.** / **I'LL BE GOING HOME NOW.**

I did get one e-mail from a ballerina who wanted to buy the original ballerina strips. I don't sell my strips, but I was flattered that there was at least one other person who liked the character. So take that, all you non-ballerina people.

WHAT ARE YOU DOING, PIG? / **BEING POPULAR.**

WHAT MAKES YOU THINK YOU'RE POPULAR? / **I'M SITTING IN THE POPULAR TREE.**

IT'S CALLED A POPLAR TREE.

MIND HELPING ME DOWN SO I DON'T GET A BOO-BOO?

Elly Elephant
wanted
romance.

She wanted a knight.
She wanted brave.
She wanted bold.

She wanted Cary Grant.
She wanted held hands.
She wanted Central Park
in the rain.

She wanted intelligence.
She wanted depth.
She wanted books read together
with tea by the fire.

9/13

She wanted passion
and surprise.
Tuxedos
and bow ties.
Truth and
not the lies.
Hellos and
not goodbyes.

One embrace that
never dies.
To the tune of
heartfelt sighs.
All lost in
deep brown eyes.
Uninterrupted
by the cries...

of

"OPEN YOUR #%&$#%# EYES,
REF!"

Elly Elephant settled
for chocolate and
a romance novel.

Elly may be my only truly sympathetic female character.

19

WHAT ARE YOU DOING, RAT?

I'M JOHNNY MIGRAINE, REBELLIOUS PUNK SUPERSTAR, HERE TO TOUR THE STATES.

OH, GREAT...AND HOW DO YOU REBEL?... BY TRASHING YOUR HOTEL ROOM LIKE EVERY OTHER 'REBELLIOUS' BAND?

BY KEEPING IT TIDY.

OKAY, THAT IS KINDA REBELLIOUS.

ROCK AND ROLL, BABY!

That is the best toilet scrubbing brush I've ever drawn.

SO YOU STARTED A PUNK BAND.

YEP. 'JOHNNY MIGRAINE AND THE BIG DOGS O' DOOM.'

'BIG DOGS'? AS IN GERMAN SHEPHERDS OR ROTTWEILERS OR SOMETHING?

NO.

But I do not draw good hot dogs. I should have at least had the wiener stick out beyond the end of the bun. My, that sounds obscene.

HOW'S YOUR BAND GOING, RAT?

I DID SOME RESEARCH. I FOUND THAT ALL GREAT BANDS HAVE DEAD DRUMMERS...THE WHO...LED ZEPPELIN...YOU GET THE IDEA.

SO WHAT'S THAT MEAN?

IT MEANS IF JOHNNY MIGRAINE AND THE BIG DOGS O' DOOM ARE GONNA BE GREAT, WE GOTTA START WITH A DEAD DRUMMER.

WHICH IS NOT REALLY THE TOUR EXPERIENCE I HAD IN MIND.

BONGO! WE DON'T TALK!

Some company actually produced a line of *Pearls* dental reminder postcards, although I have to admit I never saw any dentist actually send out one of them. The only comic strip character I've ever seen on the ones I get is Garfield. That hurts.

I recently co-wrote an animated *Peanuts* special called *Happiness Is a Warm Blanket, Charlie Brown*. The director of the special was from Pixar. I really should have pitched him my Tipsy idea.

Although I try and try, I can never draw a good monkey. This is frustrating, as monkeys are comedy gold.

I really liked this cactus character. I think I got the name "Kiko" from the title of a Los Lobos album.

Inspired by the furniture in *Calvin and Hobbes*, I tried to bend the shape of the bookshelves here. Makes it look a bit more like it belongs in a comic strip.

Guard Duck has basically two poses: right profile and left profile. I don't think I could draw him facing forward if I tried.

If you look closely, you'll see that Goat's newspaper changes from the *Cleveland Plain Dealer* to the *Pittsburgh Post-Gazette*. I try to include the names of newspapers that I know run *Pearls*.

Any reference to the declining state of newspapers always makes the editors of a few newspapers upset. I don't do it as much as I used to because I don't want them to cancel the strip.

This really was inspired by a letter to a newspaper in Wisconsin (I think it was the *Wisconsin State Journal*). If I remember right, I think the letter-writer was complaining that *Pearls* was inappropriate for children.

If you're a true *Pearls* fan, you know that Timmy is doomed. Because Timmys in *Pearls* are always doomed.

And just like that, another Timmy is dead.

I generally try to avoid having one character speak twice in the same frame (as Goat is doing in the second panel). There's just too much text and it looks messy. But at the same time, I didn't think Goat's "Who told you that?" line merited its own panel. These are the kind of nerdy things you worry about when you do a comic strip. And that is why I am now sitting behind the "Uncool" fence.

"Nerdify." What a great word. I want full credit for that one.

I can't explain it, but the word "munchies" makes me cringe. It's too cutesy or something. While we're at it, I also hate the phrase "refreshing beverage." By the way, now might be a good time to mention that whenever I make a comment in a treasury like this, I'm guaranteed to have it brought to my attention in a future e-mail. In this case, someone will almost certainly invite me to a party and tell me there will be both MUNCHIES and REFRESHING BEVERAGES.

At the time I did this strip, I drove a four-cylinder Honda. But now I drive a six-cylinder Honda. So no more "uncool" fence for me.

Reed Jackson really is my editor. He's great. Though I have to say that or he'll delete the comment.

I have killed Dilbert more than once in my comic strip. I even killed him once in *his* comic. That occurred when Scott Adams let me draw Dilbert for the day and I chose to draw him dead in a coffin.

STORY UPDATE

Rat sent Guard Duck and Mr. Snuffles to the United Feature Syndicate office in New York to take out Reed Jackson, the editor of "Pearls Before Swine." But due to an unfortunate case of mistaken identity, Mr. Snuffles and Guard Duck killed Dilbert.

If I remember right, I believe I e-mailed Scott Adams and asked him which of his characters would care the least if Dilbert died. He told me the Pointy-Haired Boss and Alice. So I included both of them here and threw in Catbert.

WHERE WERE YOU YESTERDAY?

I TRAVELLED TO NEW YORK AND SNUFFED OUT THE EDITOR OF 'PEARLS BEFORE SWINE.'

WHAT?? WHY'D YOU DO THAT?

WELL, ORIGINALLY, I WANTED TO DO IT SO WE'D HAVE NO EDITOR AND COULD DO WHATEVER WE WANT IN 'PEARLS,' BUT AFTER I GOT THERE, I CHANGED MY MIND.

WHAT DO YOU MEAN, 'CHANGED YOUR MIND'?

WELL, AFTER I KNOCKED THE POOR GUY SENSELESS, I NOTICED HIS COMPUTER HAD ACCESS TO THIS DATABASE WHERE EVERY SYNDICATED CARTOONIST IN THE COUNTRY SUBMITS THEIR WORK.

SO?

SO IT MEANT I COULD MESS WITH OTHER CREATORS' COMIC STRIPS.

10/11

YOU DIDN'T.

I DID. I DELETED CAPTIONS AND REPLACED THEM WITH SOME QUOTES I FOUND IN THIS LITTLE BOOK I CARRY AROUND.

'THE COMPLETE SPEECHES OF BENITO MUSSOLINI'??

WHAT'S WRONG WITH THAT?

"Let us have a dagger between our teeth, a bomb in our hands, and an infinite scorn in our hearts."

When I was a student in Berkeley, I bought a little book of speeches by Mao Tse-Tung. When I returned home to my conservative hometown of San Marino, California, I would carry it in my pocket and pull it out when somebody asked me a question. That concerned them.

Man, I wish I could draw a decent monkey.

CROCUS LAZYBUTTUS

THANKS FOR TAKING ME TO THE ZOO, MOM. THE NEW BEAR EXHIBIT IS AMAZING. IT'S LIKE YOU'RE IN THE WILD WITH THEM.

YES...ZOOS NOW STRIVE TO PUT ANIMALS IN AS CLOSE TO THEIR NATURAL ENVIRONMENT AS POSSIBLE. THAT WAY, YOU SEE THEM AS THEY ARE AND THE ANIMAL IS MORE COMFORTABLE.

LET'S KEEP MOVING, SON.

HEY, IT'S DAD WITH A SNOUT.

I sometimes see Larry as the Homer Simpson of *Pearls*.

MEETING OF CITY ZOO OFFICIALS

ALRIGHT, WHAT DO WE HAVE UNDER 'ANIMAL/VISITOR INTERACTION' ISSUES?

SIR, SOME OF THE BLACK BEARS HAVE LEARNED TO LEAN ON THEIR HIND LEGS AND BEG FOR FOOD, WHICH PEOPLE THROW TO THEM.

WE CAN'T HAVE LEARNED HUMAN BEHAVIOR LIKE THAT. THESE ARE WILD ANIMALS. WHY HASN'T THIS BEEN STOPPED?

FRANKLY, SIR, BECAUSE WE'VE HAD EVEN BIGGER PROBLEMS WITH THE CROC EXHIBIT.

WHAT'S GOING ON THERE?

Watch Larry chug a BEER! (one dollar)

WHAT ARE YOU DOING, PIG?

SELF-AFFIRMATION..YOU STARE AT YOUR REFLECTION IN THE MIRROR AND SAY GOOD THINGS...'YOU ARE LOVED, PIG...YOU ARE LOVED, PIG... YOU ARE LOVED, PIG.'

I FIND THAT HARD TO BELIEVE.

I WISH HE'D STOP DOING THAT.

33

The Adventures of Elly Elephant

by Rat

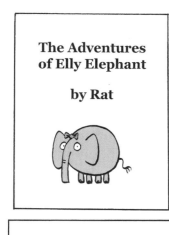

Elly Elephant played with blocks.

"With these blocks, I will build something beautiful," she said...

"I will build a block sculpture so wonderful that people will pause and weep."

"And they will hug the person next to them. And the hugs will spread."

"And there will be love."

"And wars will end. And hate will fade. And all of humankind will realize through this one work of art that they have more in common than their countries and governments and religions and traditions have led them to believe."

Elly Elephant took a break from her blocks to watch the news.

Elly Elephant played with blocks.

If I watch the news when I'm down, it really sends me into a deep depression. So I'm with Elly here.

Hello?

HI, MA'AM, THIS IS THE CITY ZOO. JUST WANTED TO LET YOU KNOW WE PICKED UP YOUR HUSBAND THIS MORNING AND PUT HIM IN THE ZOO.

WHAT?! HE'S A CROCODILE! YOU CAN'T JUST PULL HIM FROM HIS HOME AND CONFINE HIM LIKE THAT! HE'S GOT A WIFE AND A SON! WHAT'S A PREDATOR LIKE THAT GONNA DO BEHIND BARS?!

GLUG GLUG GLUG.

Watch Larry chug BEER! (one dollar)

I have never used a beer bong to drink a beer. I was always too afraid of choking and dying. Plus, I never want to die in some goofy way that will make people laugh at my funeral. Which probably guarantees that one day I'll have a piano fall on my head.

OKAY, PIG, I'VE PUT TOGETHER OUR BUDGET FOR THE YEAR. HAVE A LOOK...

Food: $4,000
Beer: $4,500
Pool table: $2,400
Flat screen TV: $2,600
Expenditures: $13,500
Income*: $25,000
$11,500 (surplus)

WOW! WE CAN AFFORD TONS OF STUFF. AND HAVE MONEY LEFT! HOW'D YOU CALCULATE OUR INCOME?

OH, I EXPLAINED IT ALL NEXT TO THAT ASTERISK BELOW.

* Rob bank

MAYBE WE DON'T NEED A POOL TABLE.

SHUT UP AND PUT ON YOUR STOCKING.

WHAT DO YOU THINK HAPPENS TO YOU WHEN YOU DIE?

GOOGLE IT.

GUYS, GOOGLE ISN'T SOME ALL-POWERFUL, ALL-KNOWING GOD...THERE ARE CERTAIN THINGS THAT NOT EVEN GOOGLE CAN HELP YOU WITH.

WHICH THINGS ARE THOSE?

GOOGLE IT.

I GIVE UP.

ALL PRAISE TO THE GOOGLE!!

This strip turned out to be *way* more popular than I ever could have guessed. Especially Pig's last line.

This was the start of probably the most artistically ambitious series I ever did in *Pearls*.

The key to being an efficient cartoonist is to write strips where you only have to draw one out of three panels.

I named these bulls after two of the cartoonists I went to Iraq with in 2009 (*Mother Goose and Grimm* creator Mike Peters and *Akron Beacon Journal* editorial cartoonist Chip Bok).

I drew each of these Alice strips while having either *Alice in Wonderland* or *Through the Looking Glass* open in front of me. I tried the best I could to imitate the cross-hatching used throughout the book illustrations, but I wasn't very good at it.

By this time, the drawings were getting much more complex and my hand was regretting that I ever started this series.

The difficult drawings culminated here in this drawing of the Raterpillar, which I think came out pretty decent.

So what do you do when you're tired of drawing a week's worth of difficult characters? Kill every single one of them.

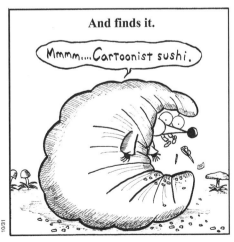

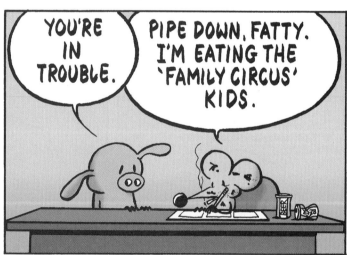

Let me say here that my mom does not smoke. Nor does she look like the woman depicted here. Nor does she like it when I do these Mom strips.

I have finally joined the Twitter revolution. I am at http://twitter.com/#!/stephanpastis

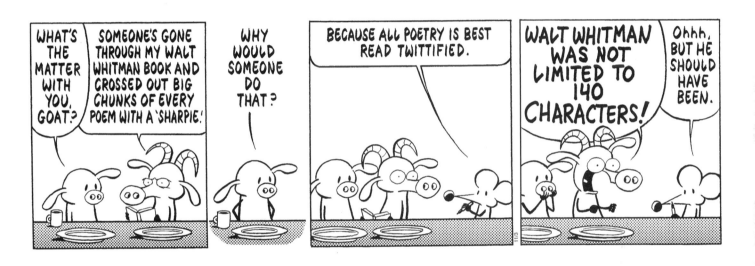

Cheese Poofs: The official snack food of *Pearls Before Swine*.

Every time my daughter Julia loses a tooth, the two of us write a letter to the tooth fairy together. And the letter is always filled with threats of physical violence. We believe that intimidation is the best approach.

Sometimes in the middle of the night I hear a sawing sound coming from our attic. I have no idea what it is. I'm guessing the rats are building something.

For those who might not know, this strip is based on the iconic Corona Beer ads that always depict two beautiful people drinking beer on some exotic beach. It never makes me want to drink their beer. But it does make me want to punch the people. Why should they get to spend all their days drinking beer on some beach while I'm slaving away writing commentary for this treasury? On a side note, since when does someone running make the sound "run run run run run"?

Did you know in Nebraska, cows outnumber people by a margin of 4 to 1? I find that frightening.

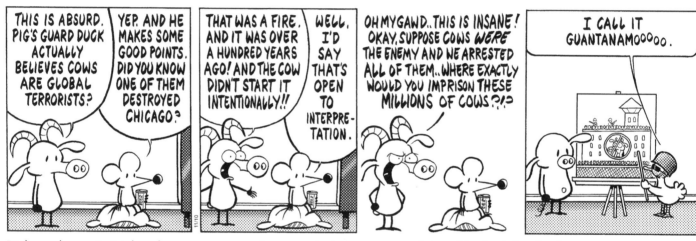

All of these cow strips were inspired by the idiotic politicians who always try to demonize some foreign culture by declaring that they "hate our freedom." Does anybody really hate someone else's freedom? Well, I guess I do. I hate the freedom of those guys in the Corona commercials.

I must admit that I, too, am an underer.

How *does* someone build a ship in a bottle? I couldn't even build one *outside* of a bottle. Heck, I couldn't even build those model cars that just required you to snap the pieces in place. I'd always end up setting fire to the thing in our fireplace.

If I remember right, I think Cathy Guisewite (creator of the comic strip *Cathy*) wrote to me to say she liked this strip. By the way, have you noticed that I say "If I remember right" an awful lot now? Clearly, I'm getting old. By my tenth treasury, I'll be saying, "If I remember right, I think I drew the comics in this book."

One of the producers of the radio show *Coast to Coast* wrote to me to say that she really liked this series. The only time I get to hear the show is when I have to get up in the middle of the night to catch an early flight. Listening to it will make you keenly aware of the type of people who are awake at three o'clock in the morning.

A callback to the earlier cow series. My, I'm clever. Excuse me while I pat myself on the back.

Dan Piraro, creator of the comic panel *Bizarro*, wrote to me to say he liked this strip. (Man, I'm dropping names big-time in these last few comments. I'll stop.)

Marco Polo wrote to me to say he liked this strip.

This was based on the fictional "death panels" that critics said were part of President Obama's health-care law. Personally, I liked the sound of them.

Strip 1 (11/23):

HEY, STEPH, IS IT TRUE THAT IN 1986, YOU WERE THE ONLY SENIOR AT SAN MARINO HIGH SCHOOL TO NOT HAVE A DATE FOR THE PROM, SO YOU SAT AT HOME AND CRIED WHILE WATCHING 'ST. ELMO'S FIRE'?

WHAT ARE YOU TALKING ABOUT? I WENT TO MY PROM.

NOT ACCORDING TO YOUR BIO ON 'WIKIPEDIA.'

PLEASE STOP ENTERING STUFF ON MY 'WIKIPEDIA' PAGE.

AND WHY'D YOU GET THE LYRICS TO 'LIKE A VIRGIN' TATTOOED TO YOUR THIGH?

For the record: 1) I *did* go to my prom; 2) I do *not* have a tattoo of the "Like a Virgin" lyrics; and 3) Well . . . I may in fact have cried while watching *St. Elmo's Fire*.

Strip 2 (11/24):

LOOK AT THIS STUDY... IT SAYS IF YOU WANT TO CONVINCE SOMEONE THAT AN IDEA OF YOURS IS WIDELY ACCEPTED, YOU JUST NEED TO REPEAT IT.

ACCORDING TO THE STUDY, AN OPINION REPEATED THREE TIMES BY ONE PERSON IS JUST AS LIKELY TO BE CONSIDERED 'POPULAR' AS AN OPINION EXPRESSED BY THREE DIFFERENT PEOPLE.....WHAT DO YOU THINK OF THAT?

RAT IS GOD. RAT IS GOD. RAT IS GOD.

WHY DO I TRY?

GIVE HIM YOUR MONEY. GIVE HIM YOUR MONEY. GIVE HIM YOUR MONEY.

Strip 3 (11/25):

JUNIOR LOST A TOOTH TODAY.

So?

SO THE 'TOOTH FAIRY' IS SUPPOSED TO COME TONIGHT AND LEAVE SOMETHING UNDER HIS PILLOW FOR IT.

Ohhh. Me get it.

WHERE YOU GOING?

To unlock front door.

THAT'S *NOT* HOW IT HAPPENS.

Ohhhhhhh. She muss use cheemney like fat guy.

50

Now that's a tooth fairy I can believe in.

Man, I could have done a ton of these letter strips. Fortunately for you, I only did three.

An homage to Abbott and Costello. If you've never seen their "Who's On First" routine, you really should Google it. It's a model of comedic writing.

I really did go to this licensing show in New York. And it really was filled with bland, big-eyed, smiling cartoon characters. It was very depressing.

I went out of my way to create the most bland, meaningless character when I created Bippy. And in one of the great ironies of my career, a cartoonist wrote to my syndicate claiming that Bippy was his character and that he had originally created it many years ago. I had no idea who the guy was or who his character was, but I felt like saying, "If you want credit for Bippy, you can have it."

I really need to get a chair like that.

I am just as nearsighted as Rat. If I try to read a book without my glasses or contacts, I have to stick my face so close to it that my nose is practically touching the page.

Perhaps the most popular pun strip to date.

These few strips were inspired by my first experience with trying to get *Pearls* made into a full-length animated movie. And truly, no one returns phone calls. Nor does what they say they will do. Nor shows up on time. In Hollywood, none of the normal rules of humanity apply.

Snuffles would be more qualified than some of the agents I met.

56

One day I just looked at *Ziggy* and noticed how odd it was that this grown man never wore pants. I mean, think about it. If you saw a guy dressed like that in a park, you'd call the police.

Apologies to the great Tom Wilson

Whenever I don't know another cartoonist well enough to believe he won't sue me, I make sure to apologize to him between the panels and put the word "great" before his name.

Panel 1:
WHAT ARE YOU DOING, RAT?

WE'RE GOING ON A HUNGER STRIKE. WE'RE NOT GONNA EAT A THING UNTIL THE COMIC STRIP CHARACTER 'ZIGGY' PUTS ON SOME PANTS.

THE ZIGGY FAST FOR PANTS

Panel 2:
YOU'RE EATING A CHEESE-BURGER.

YEAH, WELL I'M THE ORGANIZER. I HAVE TO KEEP A CLEAR HEAD. I'VE GOT OTHERS TO DO THE HUNGER STRIKE.

THE ZIGGY FAST FOR PANTS

Panel 3:
SURE HOPE HE PUTS ON PANTS.

MAY I KILL HIM FOR THE FRIES, SIR?

PEOPLE, PEOPLE, REMAIN STRONG.

STORY UPDATE

Rat has traveled to the Kansas City offices of Universal Press Syndicate, the company that syndicates "Ziggy" to newspapers, to speak to Syndicate Vice President John Glynn about putting pants on Ziggy.

LISTEN, WE APPRECIATE YOUR CONCERN, BUT ZIGGY'S CREATOR TOM WILSON, JR., HAS ASKED US TO PASS THE MESSAGE ON TO YOU THAT HE WILL NOT BE PUTTING PANTS ON ZIGGY.

OKAY... I UNDERSTAND. I APPRECIATE YOUR TALKING TO US... HEY, IS THAT AN INK STAIN ON YOUR SHIRT?

WHERE?

WHAM WHAM WHAM

MAYBE WE SHOULDN'T HAVE DONE THAT.

HEY... WE'RE SENDING OUR OWN MESSAGE.

MAY I TAKE THE CHUBBY MAN'S ¡PHONE?

John Glynn really is a vice president at my syndicate. But I try to draw him thirty pounds thinner than he really is. So if you think he's large here, you should see him in real life.

Panel 1:
OUR LONG NATIONAL NIGHTMARE IS OVER. TOM WILSON, JR. HAS AGREED TO PUT PANTS ON ZIGGY IN TODAY'S 'ZIGGY' STRIP.

YOU'RE KIDDING. WHAT'D YOU HAVE TO BRIBE HIM WITH TO MAKE HIM DO THAT?

Panel 2:
I GAVE HIM ONE OF OUR CHARACTERS. ALL HE ASKED FOR WAS SOMEONE SOFT AND CUDDLY AND CUTE THAT ZIGGY COULD SNUGGLE WITH.

OH, GREAT. SO WHAT—YOU GAVE HIM SNUFFLES THE CAT?

Panel 3:
NO NO NO...I DIDN'T GIVE HIM SNUFFLES. I MADE SURE IT WASN'T ANYONE THE STRIP WOULD MISS.

Panel 4:
THIS MAKES ME FEEL UNCOMFORTABLE.

The "long national nightmare" quote is what Gerald Ford said when Richard Nixon resigned from office.

59

LOOK, RAT, I'M COUNTING DOWN THE DAYS TO CHRISTMAS WITH MY NEW HOMEMADE CALENDAR. YOU OPEN A PRIZE BOX FOR EACH DAY THAT PASSES. IT'S CALLED AN ADVIL CALENDAR.

ADVENT.

NOW I FEEL BAD FOR FILLING THE PRIZE BOXES WITH PAIN RELIEVER.

My kids have tons of these advent calendars. But I try not to fill them with pain relievers.

WHAT ARE YOU DOING, RAT?

SPRAYING THIS POLISH ON OUR TABLES. THE LABEL SAYS IT RESTORES STUFF TO ITS 'ORIGINAL LUSTER.' I'M DONE IF YOU WANT TO USE IT.

PSSHHHHHHHH

SIGH.

"Sigh" is a great way to end a strip for which you otherwise have no ending.

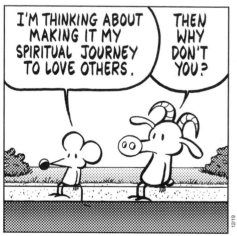

I'M THINKING ABOUT MAKING IT MY SPIRITUAL JOURNEY TO LOVE OTHERS.

THEN WHY DON'T YOU?

BECAUSE I FEAR THE MORONS WILL DISAPPOINT ME.

MAYBE YOU SHOULD START YOUR SPIRITUAL JOURNEY BY NOT THINKING OF OTHERS AS 'MORONS.'

I SEE THE TASK IS INSURMOUNTABLE.

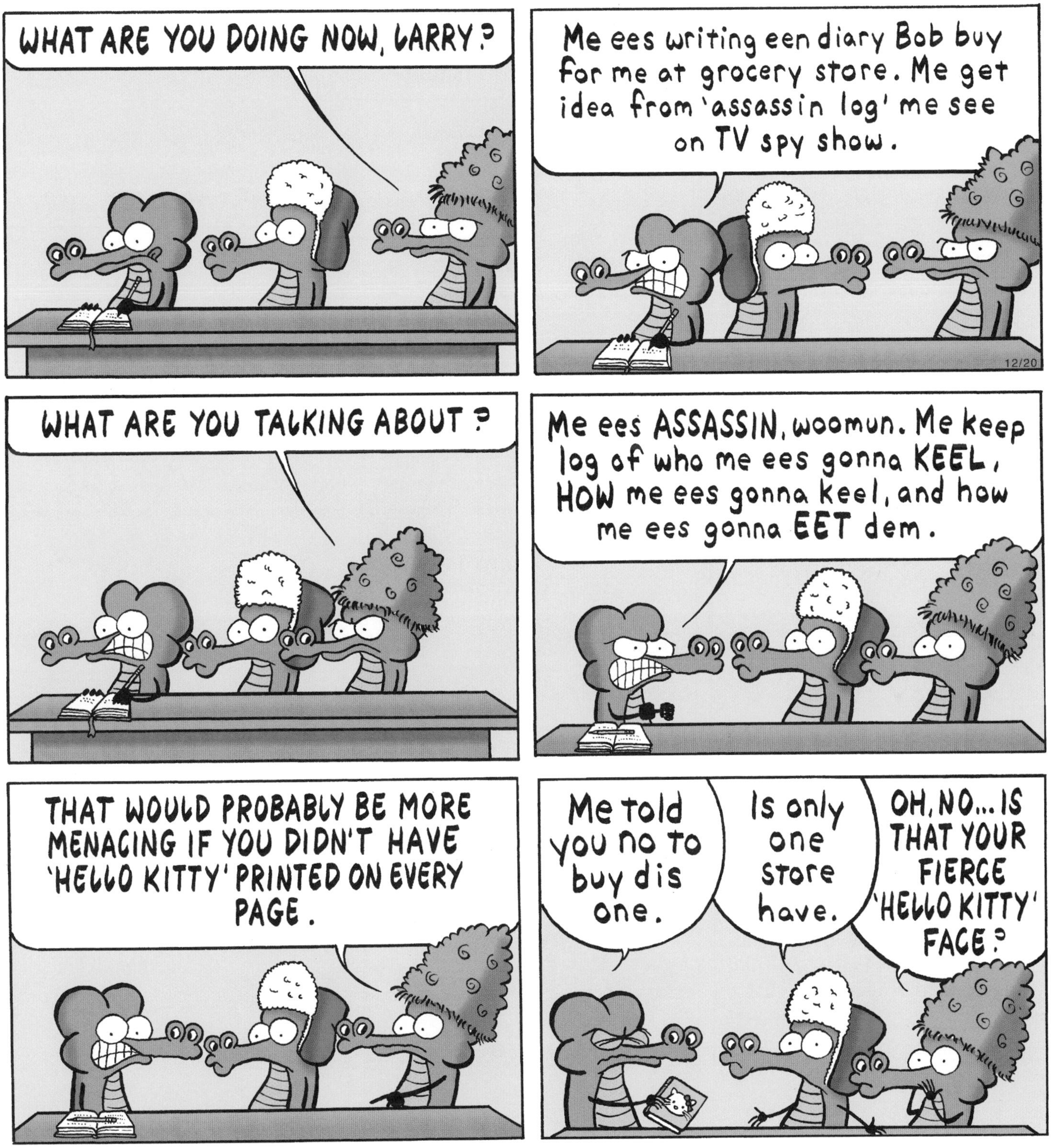
WHAT ARE YOU DOING NOW, LARRY?
Me ees writing een diary Bob buy for me at grocery store. Me get idea from 'assassin log' me see on TV spy show.
12/20
WHAT ARE YOU TALKING ABOUT?
Me ees ASSASSIN, woomun. Me keep log of who me ees gonna KEEL, HOW me ees gonna keel, and how me ees gonna EET dem.
THAT WOULD PROBABLY BE MORE MENACING IF YOU DIDN'T HAVE 'HELLO KITTY' PRINTED ON EVERY PAGE.
Me told you no to buy dis one.
Is only one store have.
OH, NO... IS THAT YOUR FIERCE 'HELLO KITTY' FACE?

Those really were the first five numbers of my cell phone number.

Really, what does that key do?

I do this all the time with my iPhone whenever I'm in a bar or a party and I'm all alone. It gives other people the impression that I'm in constant communication with many people who really, really want to talk to me. In truth, I'm playing "Fruit Ninja."

For the record, I am great at Wii golf, but I lose every single time to my son in Wii boxing. Then he brags about it. I have a very cocky son.

Assassin Log:
DAY ONE
Tooday me see TV nayture show abowt crocs.

Me see one croc who lurk all day een shallow swamp and wait for zeeba arive.

Zeeba finaly arive. He no expekk nutteeng. Croc pop out of reeds. Croc snap zeeba nekk.

Tooday me try exakk same ting.

GET OUT OF MY POOL, LARRY.

12/27

T.V. beeg fat lie.

I think I borrowed those suns and rainbows on Larry's pool from the comic strip *Rose is Rose*. That strip is as happy as *Pearls* is morose.

64

This was a good strip, but I knew that the reference to marijuana would create problems. So I hid the strip in the week after Christmas on the theory that fewer people read the comics that week. I often use that week to hide either my edgy or weak strips.

Like the marijuana strip, I knew that the notion of God's angels getting hammered could be problematic, so I put these strips in this same week.

And because this strip indirectly references sex, I hid this one here also. Too bad the week after Christmas couldn't be stretched out longer. I have a lot to hide.

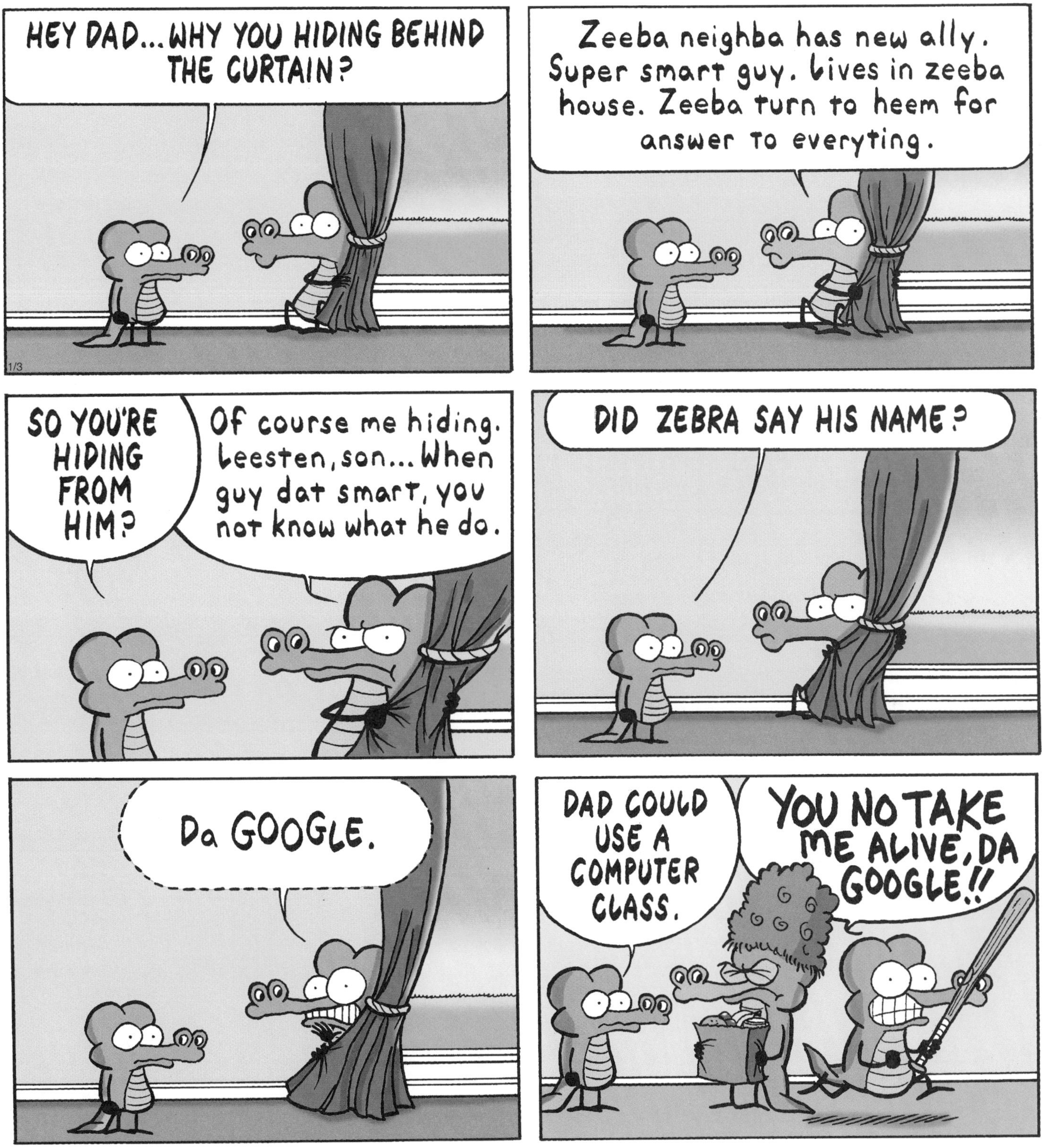
HEY DAD... WHY YOU HIDING BEHIND THE CURTAIN?
1/3
Zeeba neighba has new ally. Super smart guy. Lives in zeeba house. Zeeba turn to heem for answer to everyting.
SO YOU'RE HIDING FROM HIM?
Of course me hiding. Leesten, son... When guy dat smart, you not know what he do.
DID ZEBRA SAY HIS NAME?
Da GOOGLE.
DAD COULD USE A COMPUTER CLASS.
YOU NO TAKE ME ALIVE, DA GOOGLE!!

WHY'D YOU DRAW A LINE ON OUR FLOOR, RAT?

IT'S THE BOUNDARY OF RATOPIA, A SOVEREIGN NATION WITHIN WHICH I AM THE KING, CZAR, DICTATOR AND HEAD CHEESE.

I DON'T KNOW IF I LIKE THAT.

BOOT

WE HAVE A VERY AGGRESSIVE FOREIGN POLICY.

On the political spectrum, Rat would be somewhere to the right of Dick Cheney.

HIYA, RAT. MIND IF GOAT AND I WATCH T.V.?

I DO. I'VE ANNEXED THE T.V. SITTING AREA AS PART OF RATOPIA... I NEEDED A BUFFER STATE.

A BUFFER STATE? WHY IS IT CALLED A BUFFER STATE?

BECAUSE I AM BUFFER THAN YOU, AND IF YOU TOUCH IT, I SHALL PUNCH YOU.

THAT IS NOT THE MEANING OF BUFFER STATE.

DO I SENSE AN INTERNATIONAL INCIDENT?

C'MON, GOAT... LET'S GO FIND WIMPY-LAND.

WHAT ARE YOU DOING, LARRY?

Larry hiding. Zeeba neighba have new all-knowing ally called Da Google.

GOOGLE?! GOOGLE'S A SEARCH TOOL.

Dat why me *HIDING*.

I'M MOVING IN WITH MY MOTHER.

HA! Da Google still find you.

I have to admit, I Google myself rather often. My, that sounds inappropriate.

I think Scott Adams (creator of *Dilbert*) wrote to me once to applaud my getting away with a kick to the oompa loompas. I guess it wasn't something cartoonists felt they could do. I am proud of my pioneering ways.

That is a well-drawn sledgehammer. And when I say well-drawn, I mean that you would never confuse it with, say, a chair.

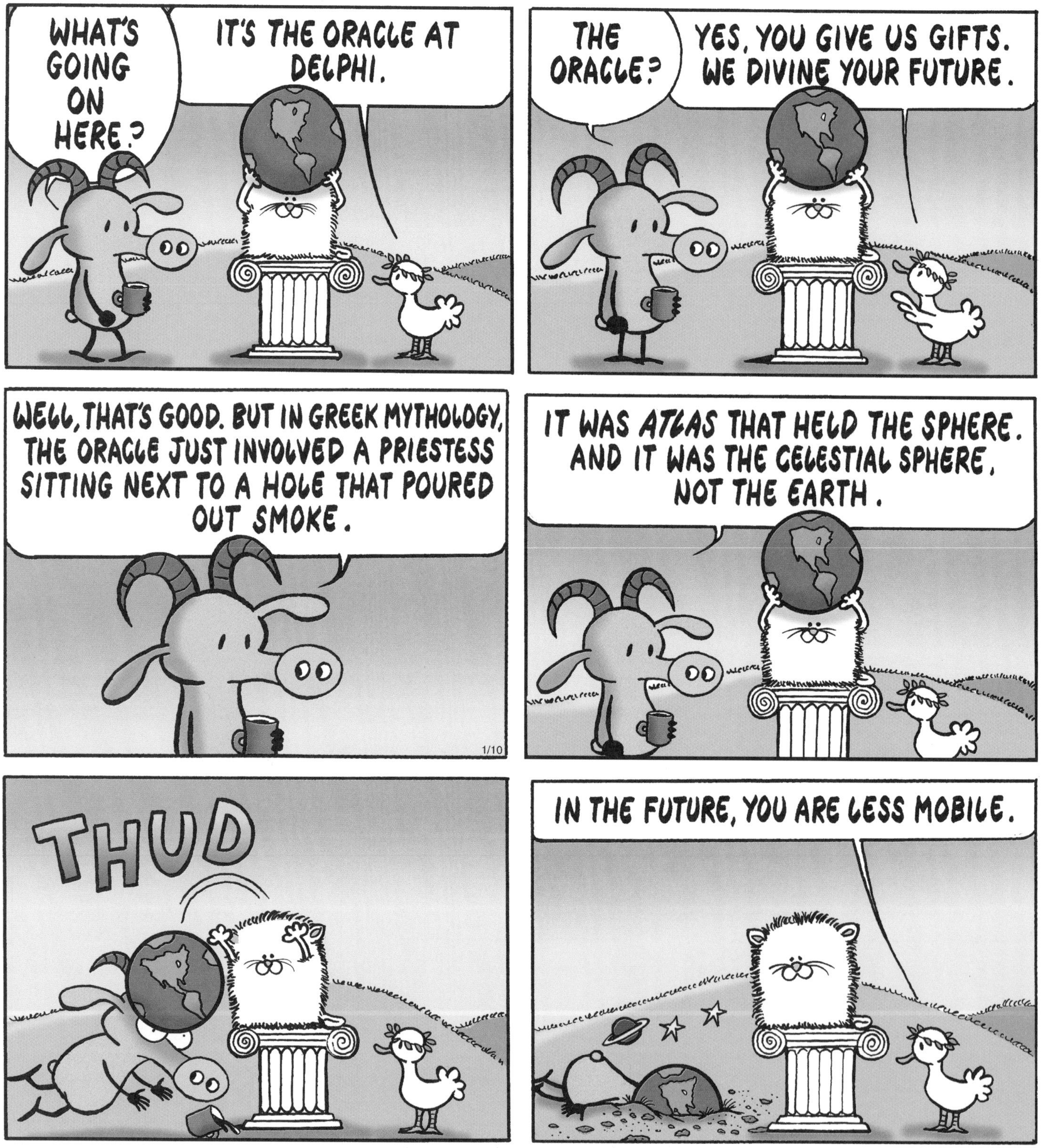
WHAT'S GOING ON HERE?
IT'S THE ORACLE AT DELPHI.
THE ORACLE?
YES, YOU GIVE US GIFTS. WE DIVINE YOUR FUTURE.
WELL, THAT'S GOOD. BUT IN GREEK MYTHOLOGY, THE ORACLE JUST INVOLVED A PRIESTESS SITTING NEXT TO A HOLE THAT POURED OUT SMOKE.
1/10
IT WAS ATLAS THAT HELD THE SPHERE. AND IT WAS THE CELESTIAL SPHERE, NOT THE EARTH.
THUD
IN THE FUTURE, YOU ARE LESS MOBILE.

My characters' arms are definitely too short for their bodies.

I think I got the idea for this series from watching those nature documentaries of rhinos that stand around all day with birds on their back.

Have you ever noticed that all of my bushes look alike? Just sort of a lump with random leaves pasted on. Perhaps one day I will learn to draw more than one variety of bush.

I think Larry's last line here is actually funnier than the punch line in the third panel.

My, this strip has a lot of profanity. I think I've offended myself.

I once read a huge book that identified hundreds of different birds and explained all of their different physical traits. I read it because I wanted to be able to see a bird in nature and know what it was. Here is the sum total of what I now remember from that book: Owls have big eyes.

I didn't get a lot of response to Katie the Drama Cow when she was first introduced. But I have since gotten a lot of requests to bring her back. So maybe she'll make a return appearance one day.

I just realized that to read Drama Cow's dialogue, you have to keep spinning the book around in circles. That's very annoying.

Neighbor Bob is not treated well in my strip. He really should move.

Danny Donkey
hated
people.

He hated their greed. He hated
their pettiness. He hated
their pigginess.

But most of all, he hated that
there were 6,000,000,000
of them.

So Danny Donkey visited
a spiritual guru.

"Climb a great mountain with a
group of strangers," said the
spiritual guru, "The shared
challenge will bring you a
new perspective."

So Danny Donkey climbed
to the top of Mount Everest
with a group of five
strangers.

And
pushed
them
off.

THIS IS 'DANNY DONKEY'S GUIDE TO SPIRITUAL FULFILLMENT':

"'YAY,' SAID DANNY, 'ONLY 5,999,999,995 TO GO.'"

I AM SO FULFILLED I COULD CRY.

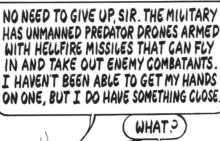

"Helikitty With a Hand Grenade" would make a great children's toy.

Actually, there are fewer than four hundred Socorro Mockingbirds left in the world. Not quite sure why I felt the need to lie. I suggest you not listen to me when it comes to facts.

My, that would be a small cow. He's not much bigger than a rat. That would really affect the world's milk production.

WHATSA MATTER WITH YOU?

I'M TRYING TO WATCH 'GONE WITH THE WIND,' BUT IT'S INTERRUPTED BY TONS OF COMMERCIALS FOR THIS GUY'S USED CAR LOT.

OH YEAH...THAT'S THAT CHINESE GUY, FRANK LEE.

YEAH, I KNOW. AND APPARENTLY, HE LOVES THE HOOVER DAM.

WHY DO YOU SAY THAT?

IF YOU BRING IN A MINIATURE MODEL OF THE HOOVER DAM, HE'LL GIVE YOU A DISCOUNT ON YOUR CAR. HIS SLOGAN IS, "YOU BRING US A DAM...WE'LL GIVE YOU A CAR."

THAT'S ODD. CAN ANYONE GET THE DISCOUNT?

NO. HE'S REAL BIG ON FIGHTING DRUG ABUSE. SO IF YOU USE DRUGS, YOU CAN'T TAKE ADVANTAGE OF THE OFFER. IT'S EVEN PART OF HIS NEW SLOGAN.

1/31

WHICH IS WHAT?

"FRANK LEE'S CAR LOT.... HIGH? DON'T GIVE A DAM."

FIRST OFF, IT'S "FRANKLY, MY DEAR," NOT "FRANKLY, SCARLETT."

SHHH... NO ONE WILL NOTICE.

S.PASTIS

After I had already written this entire strip, I found out I had gotten this *Gone With the Wind* quote wrong. But I didn't want to lose all the work I had put into this. So I tried to save the strip by including Rat's correction of me in the last panel. Here's a cartooning tip: If you're going to spend three hours writing a strip about a movie quote, first look up the movie quote.

I really did cut this bicycle image out of one of my *Baby Blues* books. My son was reading it the other day and asked, "Dad, why did you cut out part of this book?" I said, "It had some inappropriate content I didn't want you to see."

Unlike the Socorro Mockingbird lie, this fact about swans mating for life is actually true. Though I don't think they sit around on living room furniture discussing it.

This is a reference to the song "Revolution 9" on the Beatles' White Album. The song will make you want to pull your ears off.

Believe it or not, this fact about Icelanders is true. I'd make fun of them, but 11 percent of my fellow Americans believe that Elvis Presley is still alive.

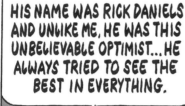

I drew this strip the day after Rick died. And it's hard for me to look at it without crying. So I'll just say that I wish you all could have known him.

HEY, MAX AND ZACH... WHERE'VE YOU BEEN?

AKRON...VISITING RELATIVES. WHAT A PAIN A PRIDE CAN BE. THEY EVEN MADE US BRING ONE OF OUR COUSINS BACK WITH US.

OH, YEAH? WHO?

HIS NAME'S 'LUCKY.' OUR FAMILY DIDN'T WANT HIM...MOSTLY BECAUSE OF HIS HUNTING STYLE.

WHAT'S WRONG WITH HIS HUNTING STYLE?

CLOSER....CLO-O-O-SER.

I chose Akron because that's where my dad grew up. My grandfather owned a pool hall there during the Depression.

ZEBRA MEETS LUCKY, THE NEW LION

YO. WASSUP?

NOTHING.

HOW 'BOUT A MAN HUG?

NO.

HUNTING'S HARDER THAN IT LOOKS.

YOU EVER NOTICE HOW POTATO CHIP BAGS HAVE THIS L'IL DOTTED LINE AND 'TEAR HERE' WRITTEN ON THE PACKAGE?

YEAH. THAT'S SO WE KNOW HOW TO RIP IT OPEN. WHY?

BECAUSE MY GIRLFRIEND PIGITA JUST BROKE UP WITH ME.

SO?

SO I THINK I MUST HAVE ONE OF THOSE PRINTED OVER MY HEART.

HAVE A BEER, BUDDY.

WAIT. THAT'S JUST A MOLE.

A very rare demonstration of kindness on the part of Rat. I feel I have to show that side of him every few years to answer the question, "Why would Pig be friends with this guy?"

Jellyfish also have no brain, which is something they have in common with Pig. Awwww. Poor Pig.

That would make a great Valentine's Day card.

84

This is a common scenario in my home. My wife, Staci, thinks of something very clever and thoughtful to give me for Valentine's Day and I have to rush to the store because I forgot what day it was. On a positive note, at least I didn't buy her a card that said, "I feel nothing."

WHAT'S THE MATTER WITH YOU, DAD? Woomun mad. Larry screw up Valeentine Day or someting.

MAKE IT UP TO HER... COMPLIMENT HER FOR NO REASON.

For no reason, me tink you not fat.

So much for you help.

The Two-Step Guide to Drawing Patty: 1) Draw Larry; 2) Add hair.

WHAT'S WITH THE TAMBOURINE, DAD? Me writing song for you muhder. Geet me out of doghouse me een seence Valeentine Day feeasco. Song tell her how unique she ees.

OH, WOW, DAD...WOMEN LOVE THAT...WHAT'S IT CALLED?

'Woomun, you not normal.'

MAYBE WE COULD REPHRASE THAT. Hmm. How 'bout, 'Woomun, peese seek profesunal help.'

HEY, MOM, WHERE'S DAD? I KICKED HIM OUT OF THE HOUSE. I COULDN'T TAKE HIM ANYMORE.

KICKED HIM OUT? HOW CAN YOU DO THAT? WHERE WILL HE STAY?! WHO KNOWS? ALL I KNOW IS *HE* DIDN'T SEEM WORRIED ABOUT IT...HE SAID TOUGH GUYS LIKE HIM ALWAYS LAND ON THEIR FEET.

BUT I DON'T WANT TO HAVE A PAJAMA PARTY.

I thought the little *Hello Kitty* doll was a nice touch.

86

Speaking of old people and tennis balls, I was walking by a tennis court the other day when one of the elderly women playing hit the ball over the fence toward me. I was going to get it for her, but then it rolled down into a little ditch. So I pretended like I didn't see what had happened and walked away as quickly as I could.

I had a friend who used to live near an arboretum filled with peacocks. And those things make the most annoying noise you've ever heard. If you don't believe me, go on YouTube and enter "noisy peacocks." Trust me, their pretty little feathers do not make up for it.

Okay, it's bad form to say you laugh at your own stuff, but this one still makes me laugh. So there.

Perhaps if newspapers fail, I really will hold a pledge drive. So please, give generously.

This was going to be a much longer series, but I got bored after two strips and stopped. It was a rather abrupt end, given that in this strip, I left readers with the impression that Rat would now be rich. So if you'd like, draw the next few strips yourself and glue them in here.

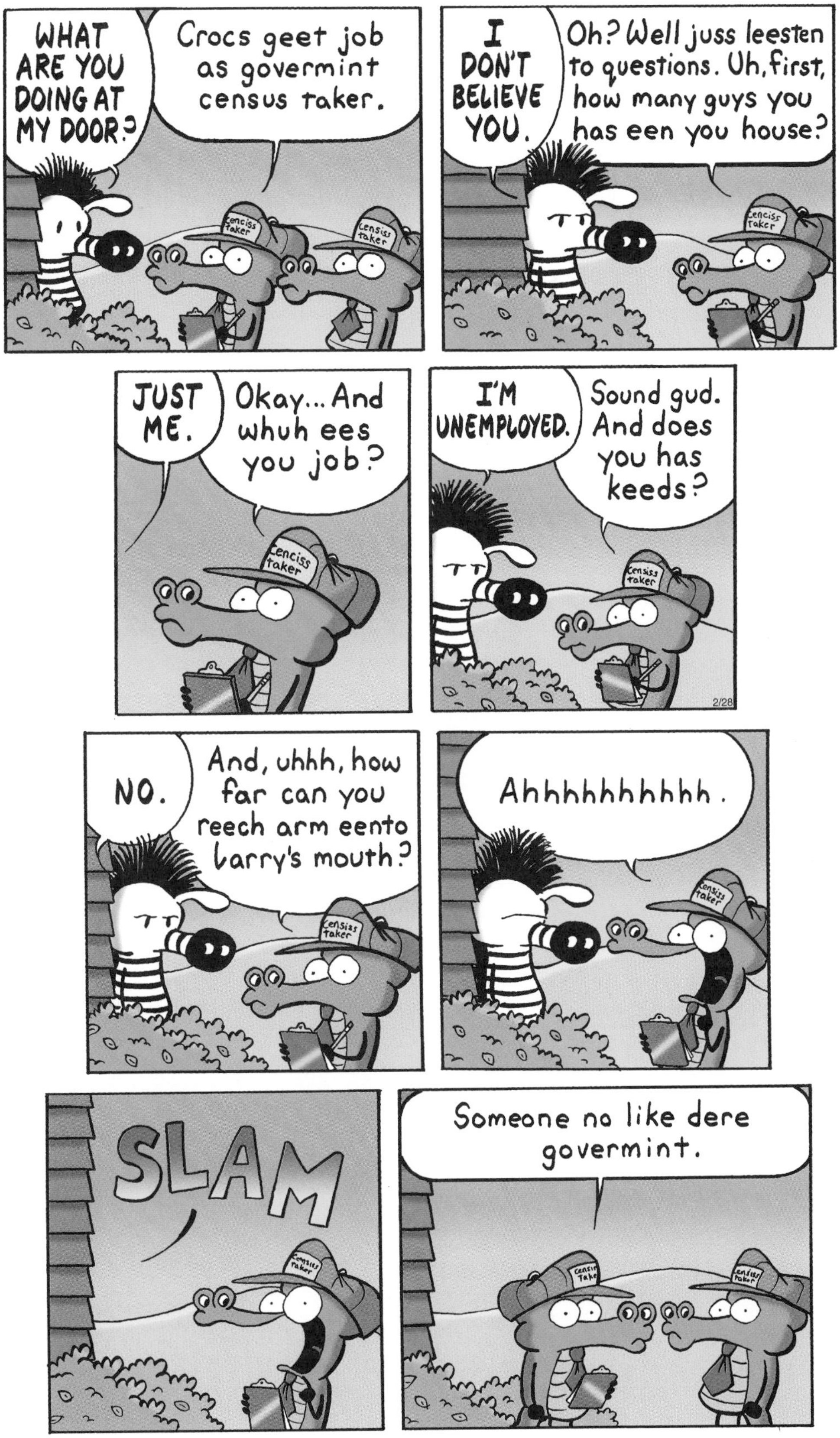
WHAT ARE YOU DOING AT MY DOOR?
Crocs geet job as govermint census taker.
I DON'T BELIEVE YOU.
Oh? Well juss leesten to questions. Uh, first, how many guys you has een you house?
JUST ME.
Okay... And whuh ees you job?
I'M UNEMPLOYED.
Sound gud. And does you has keeds?
NO.
And, uhhh, how far can you reech arm eento Larry's mouth?
Ahhhhhhhhhh.
SLAM
Someone no like dere govermint.

HEY, PIG, WHERE WERE YOU?

INTERVIEWING FOR THE 'FRIENDLY GREETER' JOB AT WALMOTOPIA. YOU KNOW, THE GUY WHO SMILES AND SAYS HI TO PEOPLE WHEN THEY WALK IN THE STORE?

OH, PIG, YOU'D BE PERFECT! WHO IN THE WORLD COULD CLAIM TO BE BETTER SUITED FOR THAT THAN YOU?

I ADORE HUMANITY.

WALMO

I think store greeters are supposed to give you a good first impression of a store. They have the opposite effect on me. They make me want to hide behind the Fritos display.

DID GOAT TELL YOU I INTERVIEWED FOR THE 'FRIENDLY GREETER' JOB AT WALMOTOPIA?

THAT'S GREAT. YOU THINK YOU'LL GET IT?

I DUNNO. THEY ASKED WHAT MY BIGGEST REGRET WAS IN TERMS OF HOW I RELATE TO PEOPLE AND I TOLD THEM THAT SOMETIMES OTHER PEOPLE MAKE ME MAD.

WHAT'S WRONG WITH THAT? IT'S HONEST. WHAT DO YOU THINK OTHER CANDIDATES SAID THEY REGRETTED?

THAT MY SHORT ARMS DO NOT ALLOW ME TO HOLD ALL HUMANITY IN ONE BIG EMBRACE.

Why do I have the characters have conversations while sitting on a curb? Perhaps they're watching a parade.

HELLO?

PIG, IT'S ME, RAT. LISTEN, I JUST WANT TO SAY I'LL BE HOME LATE. I GOT THE 'FRIENDLY GREETER' JOB AT WALMOTOPIA.

YOU? WHY'D YOU GET THE JOB?

BECAUSE I'M GOOD WITH PEOPLE. AND I KNOW HOW TO TREAT THEM. AND HOW TO WELCOME THEM.

PARDON ME, BUT I'M LOOKING FOR—

YO. BIG BONES. CAN YOU SEE I'M ON THE PHONE?

MAYBE I SHOULD LET YOU GO BACK TO YOUR FRIENDLY GREETER JOB.

HANG ON, PIG...I'M SHOVING A FAT GUY OUT THE DOOR.

92

Hullooooooooo.

Walmotopia's Friendly Greeter says, "Hi." But he is trying to watch a movie on his iPhone. So please remove your chubby, stretch-pants-covered rear from his face.

GIVE ME YOUR—

No, I will not give you my manager.

RAT'S 'FRIENDLY GREETER' JOB

HEY, CAN YOU TELL ME WHERE THE SHOES ARE?

YES, WELL, I CAN SEE WHY YOU'D BE CONFUSED, SIR, AS WE'VE CRYPTICALLY HIDDEN THEM IN AN AISLE MARKED 'SHOES.'

WHERE IS THE AISLE?

IN THE STORE, SIR, WHERE WE LIKE TO KEEP MOST OF OUR AISLES.

WHERE IS YOUR MANAGER?

ANOTHER QUESTION? PLEASE, SIR, GIVE IT A REST.

I'm not sure what that boxy-looking item is on those store shelves, but there sure aren't many of them. Either the store had a huge run on that particular item or a cartoonist I know got tired of drawing them.

HI. I'M LOOKING FOR A TELEVISION.

AND I'M LOOKING FOR SOME SOLITUDE.

WHAT'S THAT GOT TO DO WITH MY SEARCH FOR A TELEVISION?

IT'S INTERFERING WITH MY SEARCH FOR SOLITUDE.

I SEE WE'RE AT LOGGERHEADS.

The store then had a huge run on these bottle-looking things.

93

That's supposed to be the comic strip *Peanuts* that Snuffles first passes over (you can just see Lucy's feet and the bottom of Snoopy's doghouse).

That Silly String was a lot harder to draw than it looks. Please take a moment to appreciate it.

I don't eat corn flakes. I eat Honey Nut Cheerios. But that didn't rhyme with "goodness sakes."

My inspiration for "Lightnin' Pigkins" was Lightnin' Hopkins, a famous blues artist.

CAN YOU BELIEVE THE NUMBER OF WOMEN THAT CAME FORWARD IN THAT TIGER WOODS SCANDAL AND CLAIMED TO HAVE GOTTEN TOGETHER WITH HIM?

YEAH, IT WAS PRETTY UNBELIEVABLE. BUT AT LEAST I THINK WE'VE FINALLY SEEN THE LAST OF THEM.

YOU DID *WHAT?!*

Legal Disclaimer: To the best of my knowledge, Tiger Woods has not actually had sex with Pigita.

HAVE YOU SEEN PIG LATELY?

NO, I——

RIIIIING RIIIIING

HEY, WHADDYA KNOW...IT'S PIG.

HEY, PIG, WE WERE JUST TALKING ABOUT YOU. ARE YOUR EARS BURNING?

OH MY GAWD, YES! I ACCIDENTALLY SHAMPOOED WITH GASOLINE!!

THIS STRIP JUST GETS STRANGER AND STRANGER.

My mom uses this expression all the time. She said it to me one time and I thought, "What if my ears really were burning?" And a strip was born.

HEY, RAT, LOOK...I WROTE A SHORT STORY.

WOW, PIG...THIS STORY IS POSITIVELY PROSAIC.

REALLY?

CARE TO TELL HIM THAT 'PROSAIC' MEANS DULL?

WHY? THE WORD SOUNDS SO POSITIVE.

"'POSITIVELY PROSAIC,' PROCLAIMS ONE READER."

96

I have yet to see this Pig image on a car or truck. So I encourage you to be the first.

I don't know about you, but there are times when my mind will just fixate on those little logos in the corner of the TV screen. So much so that I can no longer watch the program. If that wasn't a problem for you before reading this, perhaps it will be now.

I generally don't like mentioning specific dates in the strip because it means I have to run the strip at a certain time (like here, where it had to run shortly after the diary dates in March 2010). That's hard for me because I submit the strips to the syndicate many months in advance and can't always remember that a certain strip has to be run on a certain date.

Look how the name of the newspaper is different in every panel. Goat must be very well informed.

I take my son to Lake Tahoe every summer. While there, I bet on a baseball game and we watch it from the hotel room. Giving your son a gambling addiction is a good way to bond with him at an early age.

WHAT'S THAT IN YOUR EAR?

BLUETOOTH. I'VE FORMED MY OWN PUBLIC RELATIONS AGENCY, AND I NEED TO BE IN CONSTANT COMMUNICATION. THIS IS MY FIRST CLIENT, MR. G. DUCK.

GUARD DUCK? WHY WOULD YOU HIRE RAT?

I HAD A LITTLE INCIDENT, AND NOW EVERYBODY'S IN A TIZZY.

WHAT HAPPENED?

I WAS GOOFING AROUND IN AN F-16 FIGHTER JET AND I PRESSED A BUTTON I GUESS I SHOULDN'T HAVE, AND...WELL... I BLEW UP DOWNTOWN.

YOU BLEW UP—

Uh Uh Uh Uh Uh

MY CLIENT COMMENCED THE REVITALIZATION OF THE CITY'S ONCE-THRIVING COMMERCIAL DISTRICT.

SOME PEOPLE GET PERMITS.

MISSILES ARE QUICKER.

URBAN RENEWAL: IT JUST CAN'T WAIT.

3/21

HEY, PIG, WHAT ARE YOU UP TO?

OH, MAN, I'M JUST GLUED TO THE T.V.

OH, YEAH?... ARE YOU WATCHING 'ENTOURAGE' ALSO?

NO. I ACCIDENTALLY GLUED MY HEAD TO THE T.V.

I NEED SMARTER FRIENDS.

Hey, look. One of my characters actually has a television that was sold in stores within the last ten years. Unlike Pig, who still has a model from 1974.

ANNOUNCEMENT: I HAVE SEEN TWO FRENCH FILMS. FROM THAT, I HAVE CONCLUDED THAT ALL FRENCH FILMS ARE ABOUT NOTHING.

OH, PLEASE. YOU EVER THINK YOU MIGHT BE WRONG?

LISTEN. WHENEVER YOU THINK I MIGHT BE WRONG, I WANT YOU TO THINK OF HALLEY'S COMET.

WHY?

BECAUSE IT ONLY HAPPENS ONCE EVERY 76 YEARS.

ANNOUNCEMENT: I AM LEAVING.

ANYONE EVER TELL YOU YOU'RE ABOUT AS INTERESTING AS A FRENCH FILM?

I actually like French films. Although a plot would be nice now and then.

RAT GOT A JOB.

DOING WHAT?

HE'S THE GUY THAT GETS THOSE 'UNSUBSCRIBE' E-MAILS YOU SEND WHEN YOU'RE REALLY UPSET AND NO LONGER WANT TO BE ON SOME COMPANY'S JUNK E-MAIL LIST.... HE HAS TO RESPOND TO EACH ANGRY E-MAIL.

OH, YEAH? HOW'S HE RESPOND?

AH HA HA

I'm convinced that when you send an "unsubscribe" e-mail, you are actually inviting them to submit more stuff to you, because they now know your e-mail account is active and you are looking at your e-mail.

This was a very popular strip. You can never go wrong telling jokes about men losing their oompa loompas.

Eighty percent of all greeting cards are bought by women. That's why you don't see a lot of greeting cards with trucks on them.

I have to admit I don't give a lot to charity. But I do drink beer. So at least I'm doing something.

I'm Greek. And every Easter we have these contests where each of us grabs an Easter egg and smashes them into each other. If your egg cracks, you lose. The key to winning is to be the smasher, as opposed to the smashee. And that tip alone is worth the purchase price of this book.

Hey, look . . . a plate on the diner counter that is not right-side-up. That has to be some kind of milestone.

I always see Pig as a little kid.

Butts are mentioned in the 3/30 strip, the 3/31 strip, and this 4/3 strip. That's three butt strips in one week. I take pride in that.

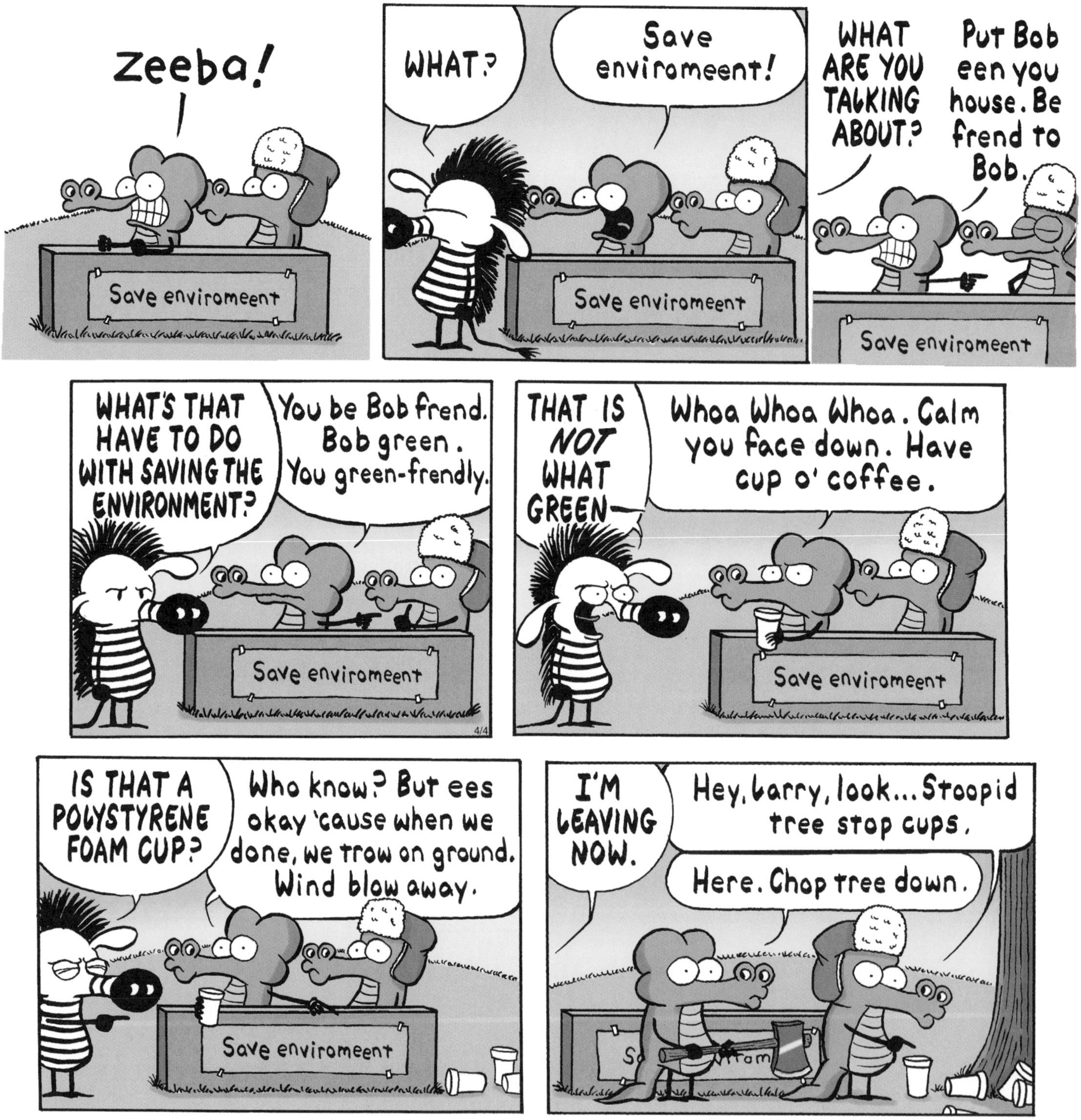
Zeeba!
Save enviromeent
WHAT?
Save enviromeent!
Save enviromeent
WHAT ARE YOU TALKING ABOUT?
Put Bob een you house. Be frend to Bob.
Save enviromeent
WHAT'S THAT HAVE TO DO WITH SAVING THE ENVIRONMENT?
You be Bob frend. Bob green. You green-frendly.
Save enviromeent
THAT IS NOT WHAT GREEN—
Whoa Whoa Whoa. Calm you face down. Have cup o' coffee.
Save enviromeent
IS THAT A POLYSTYRENE FOAM CUP?
Who know? But ees okay 'cause when we done, we trow on ground. Wind blow away.
Save enviromeent
I'M LEAVING NOW.
Hey, Larry, look... Stoopid tree stop cups.
Here. Chop tree down.

Sadly, the maker of Brillo pads did not send me any free samples for this. Perhaps they do not endorse gluing the things to your head.

This is how I play *Star Wars Battlefront* on Nintendo. I shoot everything that moves, including the guys on my own team.

It took me forty-five minutes to draw this toilet. Laugh if you must.

And it took me another forty-five minutes to figure out the sound that Pac-Man makes. "Wocka wocka" was my best approximation. If you have a better one, cross mine out and fill it in here.

Neither Dr. Seuss (dead) nor Mia Hamm (alive) contacted me after this strip ran.
I did, however, hear from a lot of Texas A & M fans.

That little window in the third panel is there to alert you it's daytime, which is when nocturnal animals sleep. Give yourself two *Pearls* points if you noticed that.

This man was a just a little doodle in my sketchbook. I liked the way he looked, so I built a strip around him.

Tubey is an actual pillow on my bed. I feel bad for him because all the other pillows on the bed are sort of square-shaped and he's this awkward cylinder. I suspect they pick on him.

I spend a fair amount of time on Skype, often talking to *Lio* creator Mark Tatulli. I also talk to his wife and kids. I'm like the sixth member of their family. At dinnertime, I've asked that he place his laptop on the dining table, so I can feel like I'm eating with them.

If you've never seen one of these walking stick insects, you really should. You can stare at an enclosure filled with them and just think you're staring at a plant. I wish I had that sort of camouflage ability when Staci makes me go to events with her family. I'd be a lamp so that nobody would talk to me.

HEY, RAT. IT'S ME, GOAT.
AHHHH...WHAT'S YOUR STUPID FACE DOING ON PIG'S NEW COMPUTER?!
BEER
IT'S '¡CHAT.' IT'S A VIDEO-PHONE.
WHY WOULD I WANT TO SEE YOUR DUMB FACE WHEN WE TALK? I DON'T EVEN WANT TO HEAR YOUR VOICE.
AWW, DON'T BE SUCH A MISANTHROPE... HEY, WHAT KIND OF BEER IS THAT?
WHAT KIND OF— ...YOU CAN SEE ME?!?
OF COURSE I CAN... IT'S A VIDEOPHONE.
AAAUGHHHHH GET OUT OF MY @#☆@☆# HOUSE!!
HEY HEY HEY... CALM DOWN. JUST TERMINATE THE CALL IF YOU DON'T—
KSSHH
IT BROKE.
4/18

I've never watched the Food Network. I don't find food compelling enough to stare at it for an hour.

My characters' relationship with clothes is very odd. Like here, where Goat puts on a coat. It draws attention to the fact that the rest of the time he must have just been sitting in Zebra's house naked. Perhaps he and Zebra are closer than I thought.

CREEEEAK
CRAAAAACK
CREEEEEEK

CRACK

CRASH!!

Me tole you skylight have weight leemit.

RAT! THANK GOD YOU'RE HOME. I NEED A PLACE TO STAY...THE CROCS FELL THROUGH A SKYLIGHT INTO MY HOUSE.

WHERE YOU LOOK-ING TO STAY?

I WAS HOPING HERE.

OH. WELL, THIS IS THE DIKEMBE MUTOMBO FINGER WAG...IT MEANS, 'GET THAT WEAK @#☆# OUT OF HERE.'

IS THAT A NO?

AND THIS IS THE RAT HIGH FIVE. IT MEANS, 'WHOA, YOU'RE NOT AS DUMB AS YOU LOOK.'

HEY. DON'T LEAVE ME HANGING.

Dikembe Mutombo was an NBA center who would block someone's shot and then do this finger wag to taunt them. I've picked it up myself and now use it against my son whenever I beat him at something. One day he'll need therapy.

YOU GOTTA LET ME STAY HERE, RAT. THE CROCS HAVE TAKEN OVER MY HOUSE. I HAVE NOWHERE TO LIVE...C'MON..WHAT ARE FRIENDS FOR?

YOU'VE STUMPED ME.

IT'S NOT A QUIZ, RAT! I'M JUST ASKING YOU FOR A FAVOR!

DOING FAVORS FOR FRIENDS IS LIKE GIVING BON BONS TO FAT PEOPLE. THEY'LL JUST WANT MORE.

YOU'RE GONNA DO NOTHING AND JUST LET ME SLEEP ON THE STREET?

THAT SOUNDS HARSH. I'LL DRIVE BY AND WAVE.

OH, JOY.

WAIT...I'M BUSY LATER. LET ME GIVE IT TO YOU NOW.

Franklin Roosevelt: "We have nothing to fear but fear itself."
Martin Luther King, Jr.: "I have a dream."
Stephan Pastis: "Doing favors for friends is like giving bon bons to fat people. They'll just want more."

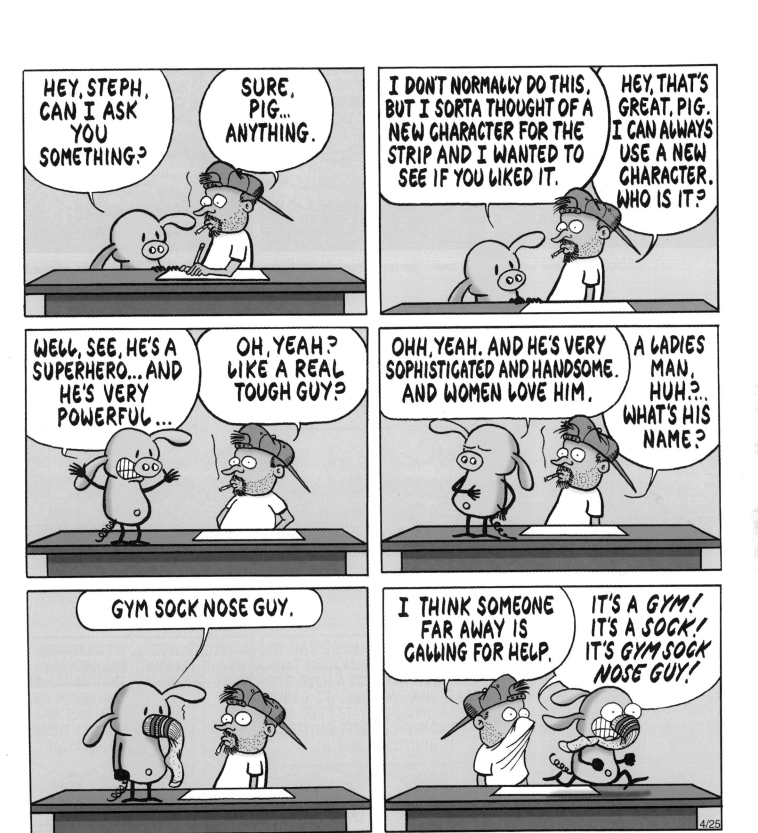

Sometimes when I wrestle with my ten-year-old daughter, I like to pull off her socks and put them on my ears. Then I roar like a genetically altered rabbit. She'll need therapy, too.

At the right edge of the panels, you can just see the beginning of graffiti that says, "Zebra sucks." I can't actually say "sucks" in the comic, so this was my subtle little way to get that in there. That sort of rebellious subterfuge is what gives me so much street cred with the homies.

I don't tend to make more coffee when I finish the pot. I try to just leave the room without anyone seeing me.

After this ran, I was contacted by someone in the U.S. military whose unit has something to do with Tomahawk missiles. They asked if they could take Guard Duck's quote from the final panel and use it on their t-shirts. I said yes.

I often put the empty box back in the cupboard. It makes my wife angry. But I don't want to make her angry. So now I put the empty box back in the cupboard and make sure she's not looking.

This was supposed to be like Peter Parker being bitten by a spider and becoming Spiderman.

I think I re-wrote the dialogue in the second panel about a dozen times. That's why the word balloons have so much empty space in them (their original dialogue was longer and took up more space). Whenever I have to start changing dialogue in a strip that has already been inked, it's a bad sign. It means the strip was probably just not funny enough. I just hate to give up on it at that point because I've already gone to the trouble of drawing it.

119

This one worked. Employees of the Sierra Nevada Brewing Company offered me everything from beer to shirts to even a two-day brewing class.

Looking at it now, those album covers all look pretty much the same. I blame that on Bach. He never put much thought into his album covers.

That drawing of me in the last panel looks very odd because for some reason I gave myself a neck. If you look at how I normally draw myself (like in the Sierra Nevada strip), I pretty much never have one. Perhaps my head is like the end of a retractable telescope, and here it was just extended.

These are truly the types of wigs worn by British judges. If I was a lawyer in Britain, I think I would spend half my time in the courtroom pointing at the judge and laughing. That would probably not help my case.

Rat's list in the second panel would be my own personal list as well. I will never in my life understand how a grown adult can watch pro wrestling. Or opera. Now if you combined the two, maybe you've got something.

Bet you didn't know spaghetti had arms.

I'm often asked how my last name is pronounced. It's PASStis. For some reason, people always want to give it a French twist and say pahSTEESE.

Hullooooo, zeeba neighba. Leesten. We crocs leetle tired you atteetude.

YEAH, WELL, I'VE HAD IT WITH YOU, TOO.

Yeah. Well, we is hate you more. So eeder you is change or Larry here write tell-all book about you and you stoopid face.

YEAH, WELL I SUGGEST YOU GET A GHOST WRITER BECAUSE NONE OF YOU CROCS IS SMART ENOUGH TO *READ* A BOOK, MUCH LESS *WRITE* A BOOK.

Ohhhhh, we no smart enough, huh? Well, dat EXAKK kind of rudeness we is talk about een book. Right, Larry?

Boo.

Dat no what ghost writer is, Larry.

Gud. 'Cause it hard to write wid sheet on hed, Bob.

Why the crocs and Zebra are sometimes separated by a bush and other times by a fence is something I can't explain. So you'll need to ask someone else.

124

Rat deserves a Nobel Prize for magically changing the name of the newspaper he is reading in each panel.

I didn't want the reader to feel sorry for the shrimp, so I gave him a pompous name: "J. Rutherford Shrimp." It engenders less sympathy than a name like "Orphan Boy Charlie."

I used to love beating my son at chess. He was only three and didn't know how to play. But still, a win's a win.

The "PBS" here is a reference to the Public Broadcasting Service, not *Pearls Before Swine*. It's easy to confuse the two. One is brilliant and informative. And the other is a TV network.

This was by far the most popular strip of the year. I guess a lot of people could really relate to it.

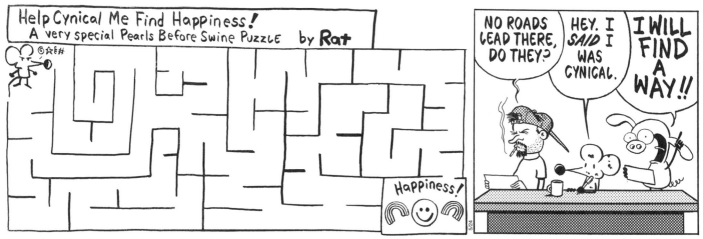

I used to do these mazes with my son. I would take a ballpoint pen and draw a line from the start straight to the end. Then he would say, "Dad, you can't go through the walls."

This was a true story. And the minute I heard it, I knew it was perfect fodder for the crocs.

 HEY, PIG, WHERE WERE YOU THIS MORNING?

 I HAD TO GO TO —

 RARE IS THE COMICS PAGE BIGFOOT SIGHTING.

 HELLO?

 HI, STEPHAN, THIS IS JEFF KEANE. I DO THE COMIC 'FAMILY CIRCUS.'

OH, HI, JEFF. HOW GOES IT?

NOT SO GOOD ACTUALLY. I'M AFRAID ONE OF MY CHARACTERS, 'JEFFY,' KEEPS GETTING HIT IN THE NOSE WITH SUNFLOWER SEEDS.

 SUNFLOWER SEEDS? WELL, THAT'S WEIRD... BUT WHY ARE YOU CALLING ME?

 BET YOU CAN'T HIT HIM IN THE EAR.

WATCH ME.

I told Jeff Keane (creator of *Family Circus*) about this strip and asked if he could put sunflower seeds in *Family Circus* on the same day this was supposed to run. And being the good sport he is, he agreed. The effect of this crossover was even better in newspapers where *Family Circus* appeared directly below *Pearls*.

 I HAVE A NEW PHILOSOPHY THAT I THINK COULD PROMOTE PEACE AND HARMONY IN THE UNIVERSE.

WHAT IS IT?

 GIVE ME WHAT I WANT WHEN I WANT IT!!!

 *THAT'S* WHAT YOU WANT EVERYONE SAYING?

NO, NO. ONLY *I* GET TO SAY IT.

129

Okay, zeeba, we crocs tired of help you geet from you mammal frends, so we geet reptile frends help keel you.

REPTILES HAVE FRIENDS?

Is you like keeding, man?... Look, Larry here have beer wid close frend, Paddy da Poison Tree Leezard.

And Burt here do high-five wid Manny da Moneetor.

And Bob here enjoy man-hug wid gud frend, Petey da —

Some frendsheeps no meant to last.

5/30

I originally drew a frog in that second panel. And as I was coloring the strip, I remembered that frogs were amphibians and not reptiles. So I added a little tail and called it a lizard.

AND THAT'S WHY I THINK DIMMY DUM FLUM HUM JIMMER JAM HOO HAW.

WHAT ARE YOU DOING, PIG?

I'M THE JIBBERISH DEBATER. WHEN MY OPPONENT MAKES A POINT, I COUNTER IT BY LAPSING INTO JIBBERISH...IT'S DISORIENTING, AND IT'S A VERY SMART STRATEGY.

I DON'T THINK IT'S SMART. I THINK IT'S STUPID.

I RESPECTFULLY CHIMMY CHONG DING DONG.

GOSH, I SURE LOVE THIS BOOK...THE AUTHOR'S A REAL MASTER OF DRAMATIC IRONY.

I'M SORRY, PIG...I DON'T MEAN TO SOUND ALL ACADEMIC...DO YOU KNOW WHAT IRONY IS?

OH, YES.

USE IT IN A SENTENCE.

THE CARPENTER'S NAIL FELT VERY IRONY.

OHH BRAVO! BRAVO!

LANGUAGES IS SORT OF MY STRENGTH.

CHECK PLEASE.

CLAP CLAP
CLAP
CLAP

I'm convinced that "ironic" means whatever you want it to mean. You can see anything and say, "Isn't that ironic?" and no one will ever call you on it. How ironic.

WHERE'S RAT TODAY?

DOING ONE OF THOSE CIVIL WAR BATTLE RE-ENACTMENTS.

YOU KNOW, THOSE GUYS TAKE THAT STUFF PRETTY SERIOUSLY. EVERY SINGLE DETAIL HAS TO BE FROM THE 1860s, FROM A SOLDIER'S GLASSES TO HIS SHOES. DOES RAT REALIZE THAT?

OF COURSE HE DOES. WHY?

NIX THE iPod.

HEY. METALLICA GETS ME PUMPED FOR BATTLE.

131

RAT'S CIVIL WAR RE-ENACTMENT

MEN, THE YANKS ARE ENTRENCHED ON THAT HILL. BUT TODAY WE CHARGE FOR CONFEDERATE GLORY. FOR OUR WAY OF LIFE, SO LET'S —

♫ Straight outta Compton, ♪ another crazy ⓒ## ☆#⑥☆ ♪ More punks I smoke, yo, My rep get bigger... ♫

I SHOULD CHANGE THAT RINGTONE.

Originally, the song in the second panel was "Big Pimpin'" by Jay-Z. The lyrics were, "We be big pimpin'/ Spending cheese/We be big pimpin' on BLAPs." But my syndicate editor told me that some of the those lyrics meant stuff that was pretty obscene. So they asked me to change it. Thus, I changed it to what you see here, NWA's "Straight Outta Compton."

RAT'S CIVIL WAR RE-ENACTMENT

YOU KNOW, I LOVE THESE RE-ENACTMENTS AS MUCH AS ANYONE, BUT THIS HARDTACK IS TOUGH TO EAT.

WELL, IT'S WHAT YOU GOTTA EAT IF YOU DON'T WANNA BE A FARB.

WHAT'S A FARB?

SOMEONE WHO'S NOT AUTHENTIC TO THE ERA. WE AUTHENTIC FOLK DESPISE 'EM.

ME TOO.

McNUGGET?

I didn't make this term up. These Civil War re-enactors really do call the non-authentic folk "farbs." Apparently, the origin of the term is from the phrase, "Far be it from authentic." That inspired me to come up with my own term for the authentic guys: Anal-retentive weirdos.

RAT'S CIVIL WAR RE-ENACTMENT

SIR, THE BATTLE'S OVER. WE TOOK THE HILL.

THE SOUTH DOESN'T TAKE THE HILL IN THIS BATTLE. THE NORTH HOLDS IT.

NOT TODAY, SIR.

HISTORY SCHMISTORY.

POTUS is the Secret Service's acronym for "President of the United States." Knowing this, I thought it would be sort of fun to call a character "Potus" and see if any readers knew the acronym. Surprisingly, they did. But it then led to a whole array of speculation about who symbolized what. For example, a number of readers thought Potus was supposed to be President Obama, and that the crocs and Zebra represented Palestine and Israel. One reader wrote, "Obviously a comment on the Hamas flotilla being a peace activist disguise. Now I have to re-examine previous alligator vs. zebras strips for such subtlety."

The reason people thought this was a commentary on Israel was that Zebra was being asked to give up body parts like Israel was being asked to give up land for peace. I have to admit, the explanation made enough sense that it made me start to question whether that was subconsciously in my head when I wrote it. Maybe so. All I can tell you is that I didn't do it intentionally.

I goofed on this one by not making the labels on the peanut bags large enough to read (remember, some newspapers really shrink these strips). So a number of people wrote to me on the morning this strip appeared to ask what all those things were around the crocs' feet.

Okay, so here I have a neck in the third panel, but no neck in the first and second panels. Must be that retractable head thing again.

135

I've never read *Moby Dick*. I'd like to, but I fear that after I am done I'll want all those hours of my life back.

This turned out to very popular series.

Why are apples the fruit we give to teachers? Why not cantaloupes?

137

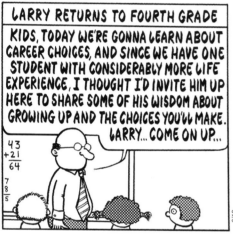

Note the accuracy of the math problems behind the teacher. Not to brag, but I did those without any help from anyone.

I'm sometimes asked if I know how many crocs have died in *Pearls*. I don't, but I'm guessing it's more than in *Ziggy*.

This was the most popular strip in the series.

Note the drawing of Elly Elephant on the wall in the second panel. Who the other guys are is anyone's guess.

OFFICER POTUS... IS IT SAFE TO BE AROUND YOU?

YEAH. BECAUSE OF MY ACCIDENTAL SHOOTINGS, THE DEPARTMENT TOOK AWAY MY GUN. NOW ALL I HAVE IS A STUPID BILLY CLUB.

WHAM WHAM WHAM

DANGEROUS LITTLE THING.

WELL, THE DEPARTMENT'S SO TIRED OF MY ACCIDENTS THEY'RE NOW TALKING ABOUT TAKING AWAY MY BILLY CLUB.

CAN I SEE IT?

SURE.

NOT WHAT IT'S FOR.

THE NAME CONFUSED ME.

I include *Family Circus* characters so often in my strip that at book signings, I'm sometimes asked to draw a *Family Circus* character instead of a *Pearls* character. The only one I can really do from memory is Jeffy, because I draw him so much. This strip marks a rare appearance by his lesser-known sibling, Billy.

I HAVE FOUNDED AN OPERA COMPANY.

YOU?...WHO DO YOU HAVE THAT CAN SING OPERA?

NOBODY.

THEN WHAT DO YOU HAVE?

A FAT GUY DRESSED FUNNY.

IT'S NINETY PERCENT OF THE BATTLE.

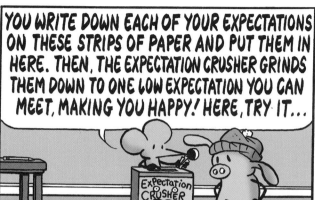

This "lower your expectations" theory is actually my wife's theory of life. Especially when it comes to vacations. She always goes in expecting the worst and then is pleasantly surprised. That's different than my experience on vacations. I go in expecting the worst and then experience a debacle even bigger than I could have imagined.

I'M STARTING TO THINK I MIGHT HAVE A STALKER. AND I THINK IT'S A SHEEP. AND I THINK SHE'S WATCHING EVERYTHING I DO.

DUDE, PLEASE. IF YOU'RE GONNA ACT LIKE A PARANOID WEIRDO, AT LEAST TURN THE OTHER WAY SO PEOPLE DON'T KNOW WE'RE TOGETHER.

I really loved this strip, but it didn't get a huge reaction. That really bothered me. So if you liked it, please let me know so we can be friends again.

HURRY UP, PIG, WE'RE GONNA BE LATE FOR THE MOVIE!

HOLD ON, RAT... I'M TRYING ON A SWEATER AND WANT TO SEE HOW I LOOK.

LIKE THE STUD YOU ARE.

DO *YOUR* WOOL SWEATERS COME WITH THE SHEEP ATTACHED?

WHAT DO YOU DO WHEN YOU GET REALLY DEPRESSED? WHEN EVERYTHING IN YOUR LIFE IS JUST TOO MUCH TO DEAL WITH?

I SHAKE MY *MARACAS*.

SHAKE-A-SHAKE-A-SHAKE
SHAKE-A-SHAKE-A-SHAKE
SHAKE
SHAKE
SHAKE

NOT A FAN?

NOT SO MUCH.

When I write at my studio/condo, I sometimes draw on the walls. One day I drew this image of Pig shaking maracas and I liked it so much, it spawned this strip.

Bet you weren't aware that a shaking maraca actually makes the sound, "shake-a-shake."

The first and second strips in this McZeeba's series were drawn many years ago. But I never really liked them, so they just sat on my shelf. But then I thought of a way to tie the strips into the Potus storyline and the sheep storyline. So I did some more McZeeba's strips and finally ran them here. I think this is the first and only time where strips in the same *Pearls* series were drawn many years apart.

144

When I originally wrote this strip, I thought it was pretty good. Then when I was finished drawing it, I really didn't like it. To me, it was just sort of flat. So I decided to run it on a holiday weekend (July 4), on the theory that fewer people would read it. But when it ran, it got a surprisingly good reaction. This proves yet again that I just never know what will work.

This was the second of the two original McZeeba's strips. The "bacon tastes good" line is an homage to the movie *Pulp Fiction*.

Some cartoonists spend months building up a marriage storyline. I do it in one panel.

If you really look at that kitchen counter in the first panel, you'll see that it only sticks out about six inches from the wall. The temptation there is to blame the cartoonist. But don't. Larry and his wife just hired a bad contractor.

147

This strip seemed like a good idea until I had to draw that Doberman ten times. And I know what you're saying to yourselves. "*That* was supposed to be a Doberman?"

148

This was a parody of that ad campaign, "Beef: It's what's for dinner."

After this strip ran, one shocked reader wrote to me to say, "She's just hurt, right? She didn't die?" To which I wrote back, "Oh, no. She definitely died."

This strip was in reference to the *Deepwater Horizon* oil spill that poured oil into the Gulf of Mexico for almost three months in 2010. Ironically, on the very day this strip appeared (July 15), the leak stopped. As one reader later wrote to me, "You spoke and the oil stopped flowing. Now ask for world peace."

It took way too long to draw each of those little bags inside the vending machine. So a series that was supposed to last a week ended after just two days. Maybe next time when I do a series centered around a vending machine, I'll just leave a large blank space in the middle of the panel and write, "Imagine large vending machine here."

Gee, my hair has a blondish tint in this strip. Perhaps I've been using peroxide.

Having go-to gags are a great luxury for a cartoonist. But they also run the risk of making the strip seem repetitive. And that's bad. Being repetitive. That's bad.

I sometimes pull my sweatpants halfway up my chest and walk around the house like that. It makes my kids embarrassed to have me for a father. I strive for that reaction.

I tried to draw the lifeguard stand facing directly toward the viewer, so I wouldn't have to draw the sides or the back. We in the industry have a term for that: laziness.

In the second panel, Rat was originally saying, "Rocking the banana hammock." But my syndicate would not let me say that, because they felt that "banana" was a clear reference to a man's private parts. I argued with my editor over this for fifteen minutes. To shame him, I said, "You realize you're the only editor in the history of comics who has censored the word 'banana.'"

We are all
Gulf
residents.

Like the 7/15 strip, this was another reference to the *Deepwater Horizon* oil spill.

I like how the back of Rat's book just has him with his arms raised triumphantly. I should do that on the backs of all my books. Wait, I put myself on the *front* of my books. Never mind.

I think poetry would be much better if it was clear and to the point. For example: "I like peas/They are green/ They are round/I like peas." Now that's a classic.

I drew the first two panels with my left hand to give it this "shaky" effect. Please tell me you noticed the difference.

My wife, Staci, read this one over my shoulder as I was drawing it. She said, "That's kind of stupid." She's kind of stupid, too, so I ignored her.

See, I can make the comment I did after that last strip because I am fairly confident my wife doesn't read these treasuries. So please, let's all agree to keep that last comment between you and me.

Hullooo zeeba neighba...Leesten...Crocs buy you ostreech egg...Ees geeft... Put een house.

WHY WOULD I WANT AN OSTRICH EGG?

Ees lotta egg. You make ommleet.

YEAH, WELL IT LOOKS A LITTLE BIG FOR AN OSTRICH EGG...HOW DO I KNOW THAT'S NOT A CROC IN THERE?

Ooh, dat very oofensive. Now you ees, like, call me liar. Mebbe you not know ostreech babies HUGE.

NO, NO, NO..I KNOW OSTRICH BABIES ARE BORN LARGE, SO IT MAKES SENSE THEIR EGGS WOULD BE LARGE. I'M JUST BEING CAUTIOUS. HERE, FORGET ABOUT IT...HAVE A BEER.

Okay. Beer make better.

WHERE MY @#☆※#T BEER?

Baby's first words.

8/1

The San Francisco Zoo once invited me to draw my characters on an ostrich egg, which they were then going to auction off. I said no. I was too afraid of dropping the egg and having the next day's *San Francisco Chronicle* read, "Cartoonist Kills Baby."

In case you can't read it, the line between the panels says, "Stephan Pastis played with *Star Wars* figurines until he was 16 years old." To the best of my knowledge, I was fifteen, so that statement is patently false.

This was another strip that I originally intended to turn into a series, but the candy house just took too much time to draw. That happens a lot with me. It's the same reason you'll never see me draw a series where a 200-piece orchestra engages in hand-to-hand combat with the entire U.S. Senate.

Searching for the Netflix envelope is the only reason I even look through our mail. I leave all the bills and stuff for Staci. She's the same person I called "stupid" about five comments earlier.

I'm gonna take this opportunity right now to formally apologize to my wife for some regrettable comments that were made earlier.

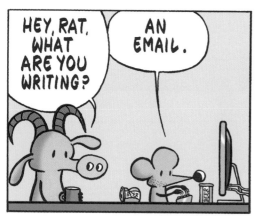

HEY, RAT, WHAT ARE YOU WRITING?

AN EMAIL.

EMAIL! EMAIL! EMAIL! DOESN'T ANYONE SEND A LETTER ANYMORE?

YO. COOL YOUR HORNS, SPAZ-BOY. I'M NOT THE BIGGEST FAN OF EMAIL EITHER. I KNOW IT'S GOT ITS PLUSSES AND MINUSES.

YOU DO?

YEAH... FOR EXAMPLE, EMAIL TENDS TO RUDIFY ALL COMMUNICATION.

RUDIFY?

YEAH... MAKES IT RUDER. MAKES NICE PEOPLE SOUND RUDE. MAKES RUDE PEOPLE SOUND RUDER.

YES! EXACTLY! AND THAT ALONE OUTWEIGHS ITS PLUSSES!

THOSE **ARE** ITS PLUSSES.

PLEASE MAKE YOUR EVIL LIPS STOP MOVING.

PREPARE FOR AN EMAIL!!

YOU LOOK GRUMPY THIS MORNING.

I AM.

DID YOU KNOW THAT IT TAKES 43 MUSCLES TO FROWN, BUT ONLY 17 MUSCLES TO SMILE?

WHAT'S IT TAKE TO PUMMEL A PERKY GUY?

YOU MAY NOT BE A MORNING PERSON.

I AM NOW. DON'T MOVE.

Every office I've ever worked in had at least one perky person who greeted me with a big chirpy "Hello" in the morning. I always wanted to say back, "I've been here one minute and already you've ruined my day."

BEHOLD! I, RAT, NOW HAVE MY OWN iPod, iPhone AND iPad.

YOU KNOW, I ALWAYS HATE HANGING OUT WITH PEOPLE WHO HAVE ALL THAT STUFF BECAUSE THEY PAY MORE ATTENTION TO ALL THAT THAN THEY DO TO THE PEOPLE THEY'RE WITH.

YES. IT IS ALL PART OF MY GRAND STRATEGY FOR SOCIAL INTERACTION WITH THOSE AROUND ME.

WHICH IS WHAT?

i Ignore.

i Give Up.

i Hugga You Make You Feel Better.

Legal Disclaimer: Apple paid me no money for this product placement. If you know how to get them to, please advise.

HEY, GOAT, IN ANCIENT GREEK PLAYS, WHAT WAS THE CHORUS?

A GROUP OF PEOPLE ONSTAGE WHO COMMENTED ON THE ACTION, USUALLY IN SONG... WHY?

♫ COMICS SHOULD BE FUNNY ♪ ♪ BUT THIS AIN'T WORTH OUR MONEY... ♫

THIS COULD GET ANNOYING.

♫ THE HUMOR'S FAR AFIELD ♪ WE PREFER 'GARFIELD' ♫

I wrote this at a time that I was reading a lot of ancient Greek plays by Sophocles and Euripides. Let me sum them up for you in two sentences: 1) People talk. 2) Everyone dies.

161

"Fanny" means something much different in Britain than it does in the United States. So the adolescent in me loves getting away with strips like this.

This strip was much more popular than I expected it to be.

162

I think I can safely say this is the first time a syndicated comic strip pig has been made to look like Bea Arthur. I hope one of you at home is keeping track of these milestones.

I have a cousin who got a whole bunch of his hair singed off by a propane barbecue. At a party later that night, a girl who had no idea what had happened complimented him on his haircut.

One time I was sitting at a blackjack table in Reno with a friend who was smoking a cigar. He won a hand and took the cigar out of mouth to cheer. When he put the cigar back in his mouth, he wasn't watching what he was doing, and put the lit end in his mouth. That made him stop cheering.

RAT OPENS AN INDIAN CASINO

SIR, WOULD YOU LIKE TO HIT OR STAY?

WELL, LET'S SEE, I'VE GOT A MR. JACK AND AN ACE...SO MAYBE I SHOULD STAY?

BLACK-JACK

OHHHHH...YOU DON'T WANT MR. JACK TO BE LONELY, DO YOU?..HE'S GOT NO PEOPLE FRIENDS.

THEN GIVE MY JACKIE PEOPLE FRIENDS!

BLACK-JACK

TWO KINGS!

SIR, YOU'RE LOSING ALL YOUR—

JACKIE'S GOT SOME PEOPLE FRIENDS!

BLACK-JACK

Whuh you doeeng, Larry?

Me hiding een zeeba garbage. When zeeba empty trash, me ees keel.

Dat great idea. Me hide een one next you.

☆◎☆#◎ YOU, ◎☆#T#☆#♂.

Dat guy reelly ees grouch.

When I was a little kid, my afternoon routine was to watch *Sesame Street*, *Mr. Rogers' Neighborhood*, and *The Electric Company*, all educational shows on PBS. No wonder I'm so brilliant today.

WHAT DO YOU GOT THERE, PIG?

IT'S MY DECEASED FRIEND, WILLY THE WOODPECKER. I GUESS HE JUST WORE HIMSELF OUT CONSTANTLY BANGING HIS FOREHEAD INTO A TREE.

WOODPECKERS DON'T USE THEIR FOREHEADS. THEY USE THEIR BEAKS.

WILLY WOULD HAVE FOUND THAT INFORMATION USEFUL.

I changed the punch line in the last panel a number of times. It originally said, "Willy fought the system."

In keeping with the somber mood of a memorial service, the croc here just says, "Hullo, zeeba neighba," as opposed to the usual, more festive "Hullooooooo, zeeba neighba." Ah, the subtleties of my craft.

This has a kinkier vibe than I intended.

The falling of the "United Feature Syndicate" copyright line was perhaps prophetic. Six months after this strip ran, the syndicate announced that it was closing its doors. *Pearls* is now syndicated by United's former rival, Universal Uclick.

A lot of people seemed to relate to this strip. As one university staff photographer wrote to me, "I spend a large percentage of my time asking female students to please NOT put their heads together when I am photographing them."

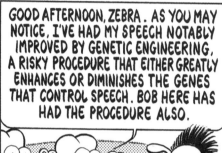

There was something about this strip that came out harsher than I intended. Almost like Pig is a Guantanamo prisoner. All I can tell you is that it was funny when it was in my head.

Danny Donkey hated life.

He hated the routine.
He hated the obligations.
He hated the cold.

So Danny Donkey went to Key West.

There, he sat on the beach. And drank.

Then one day he got a call from his mother. "Vacation is one thing," said his mother, "But you cannot live out the rest of your life drinking beer on a beach."

"Why is that?" asked Danny Donkey.

"Because life must have BALANCE," said his mother, "And GOALS. And ACHIEVEMENTS."

Danny Donkey paused. For he knew that his mother was right.

So Danny Donkey balanced a beer on his head and set a goal of throwing his cell phone into the sea, which he achieved.

KERPLUNK

I went to Key West in the spring of 2010. I have since referenced it a few times in the strip.

If you haven't noticed, all of the *Pearls* characters have siding on their house and bushes right off the porch. Some cartoonists would vary that a little.

Why do my characters talk from behind a brick wall? Perhaps they're in a minimum security prison.

Snuffles generally has no arms. But sometimes, like on the cover of *Pearls Blows Up*, I have to temporarily give him arms so he can accomplish something. I try to avoid that, though, because it always looks odd to me.

Ah, political satire. Surely, my Pulitzer Prize cannot be far off.

For the non–football fans among you, this is something that players on the Green Bay Packers football team do after scoring a touchdown on their home turf, Lambeau Field. They jump into the crowd and the crowd catches them. I'm thinking about doing it after book signings. Though I fear some of you would drop me.

Well-drawn rake. Well-drawn jar. A banner day.

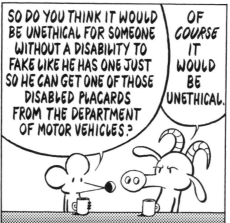

I thought Rat's comment about disabled parking spots would generate complaints, but it actually drew some support. As one reader wrote, "I am both old AND fat but I pride myself on being able to wheeze from a regular parking place to the store."

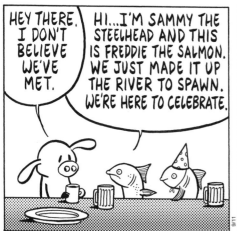

Here I both entertain AND teach you about fish. That, my friends, is what you call a multifaceted comic strip.

For those who might not have noticed, the *Jaws* poster changes from panel to panel. If you DID notice, let me know and I'll come to your house and pat you on the back.

I was surprised I got away with this one, especially after the "banana hammock" fiasco. So if you're scoring at home, please remember: You can say "booty," but never "banana."

When my son saw this strip, he said, "This is kind of stupid." He and my wife have a lot in common.

I have never attended any of my high school reunions, but I have made the mistake of looking at photos of my classmates on Facebook. And let me tell you, those people are OLD.

We had recently replaced all of the windows in our house when I wrote this strip. And if that's not fascinating, I don't know what is.

When I draw another cartoonist's characters, I really need to copy from the exact pose I want to use. In other words, I can't guess what Hagar looks like sitting at a table. I need an image of him actually sitting at a table. And in the case of this particular strip, I didn't have the poses I needed. So I took a chance and e-mailed Hagar's creator, Chris Browne, to see if I could get them. He was very kind and sent me a whole bunch of Hagar poses.

A priest in Minneapolis asked for permission to use this strip in a sermon. Perhaps he was from the Church of Cheese.

They do! They do!

My dad, who grew up in Ohio, uses the term "soda pop." But I don't think I've ever heard anyone from the West Coast say it. People here just say "soft drink."

DID YOU KNOW THAT THE WEALTH OF THE TOP ONE PERCENT OF AMERICANS IS GREATER THAN THAT OF THE BOTTOM 95 PERCENT COMBINED?

SO?

SO I'M TAKING IT BACK.

TO GIVE TO THE POOR?

WELL NOW THAT WOULD BE STUPID.

HAVE YOU SEEN MY VUVUZELA? IT'S THAT OBNOXIOUS HORN BLOWN BY ALL THOSE FANS DURING THE WORLD CUP.

WHY'D YOU BRING IT HERE?

BRRRRFFF

CELL PHONE BLABBERS BEWARE.

The perfect instrument for Rat.

HEY, RAT... I'D LIKE YOU TO MEET MY FRIEND, FOOFY THE FLYING FISH.

FLYING FISH CAN'T REALLY FLY. THEY'RE JUST CALLED THAT BECAUSE THEY LEAP OUT OF THE WATER, GIVING THE ILLUSION OF FLIGHT.

PLOP

FOOFY DIDN'T NEED TO KNOW THAT.

Pearls Rule No. 55: Characters with cute names like "Foofy" will always die.

I really liked the way this strip came out.

Reversing the view on the last panel is something I do more and more now. I do it whenever there's a switch in the order the characters speak. In other words, Rat speaks first in panels 1 through 3, but in the final panel Goat speaks first. I can't just have them switch seats. So I reverse the angle.

To accurately draw Sean, I simply took my shirt off and looked in the mirror. Then I ignored my belly and pretended I had muscles.

Those are stained glass windows in the background. I say that because they look more like windows that have been shattered by an angry mob.

I never hear anyone use this expression anymore. I'm gonna take credit for that.

Are there any other comic strip characters that lack a nose?

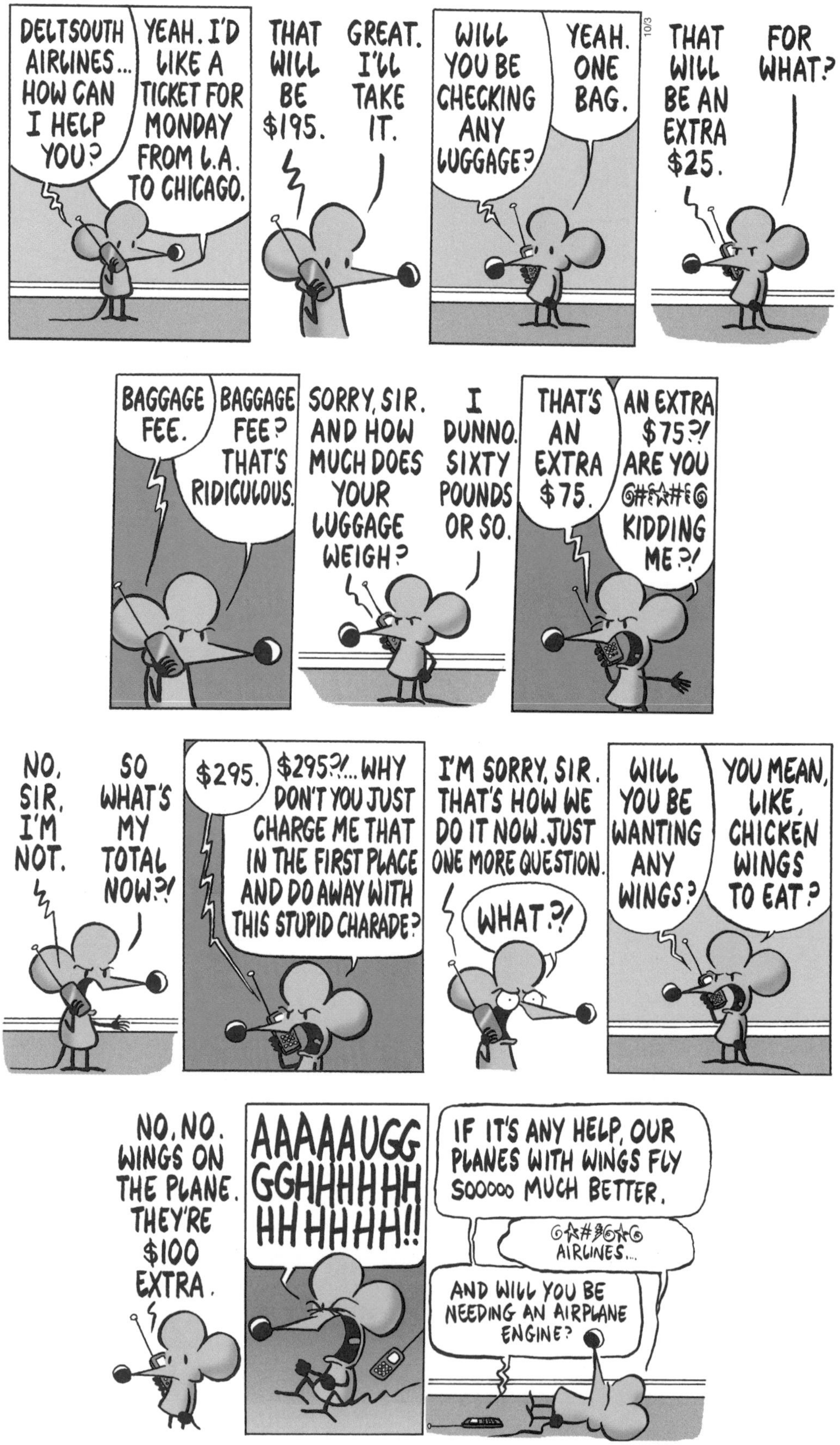
DELTSOUTH AIRLINES... HOW CAN I HELP YOU?
YEAH. I'D LIKE A TICKET FOR MONDAY FROM L.A. TO CHICAGO.
THAT WILL BE $195.
GREAT. I'LL TAKE IT.
WILL YOU BE CHECKING ANY LUGGAGE?
YEAH. ONE BAG.
10/3
THAT WILL BE AN EXTRA $25.
FOR WHAT?
BAGGAGE FEE.
BAGGAGE FEE? THAT'S RIDICULOUS.
SORRY, SIR. AND HOW MUCH DOES YOUR LUGGAGE WEIGH?
I DUNNO. SIXTY POUNDS OR SO.
THAT'S AN EXTRA $75.
AN EXTRA $75?! ARE YOU
KIDDING ME?!
NO, SIR, I'M NOT.
SO WHAT'S MY TOTAL NOW?!
$295.
$295?!... WHY DON'T YOU JUST CHARGE ME THAT IN THE FIRST PLACE AND DO AWAY WITH THIS STUPID CHARADE?
I'M SORRY, SIR. THAT'S HOW WE DO IT NOW. JUST ONE MORE QUESTION.
WHAT?!
WILL YOU BE WANTING ANY WINGS?
YOU MEAN, LIKE, CHICKEN WINGS TO EAT?
NO, NO. WINGS ON THE PLANE. THEY'RE $100 EXTRA.
AAAAAUGGGHHHHHHHHHHHH!!
IF IT'S ANY HELP, OUR PLANES WITH WINGS FLY SOOOOO MUCH BETTER.
AIRLINES...
AND WILL YOU BE NEEDING AN AIRPLANE ENGINE?

I'd like to say I wrote this after reading Ray Bradbury's *Fahrenheit 451*. But the truth is I wrote it after watching the movie version on a wall-size TV.

I wrote this series after hearing that Cathy Guisewite, the creator of *Cathy*, was retiring.

These strips were tough to draw because as I mentioned earlier, I need to copy from exact poses when I parody other characters. And obviously, there were no poses available of a deceased Cathy floating through space.

I really liked the way this pose of Cathy came out. It's hard to keep the essence of a character when you change them that drastically. But here, Cathy's eyes are so iconic that you still know it's her.

After the *Cathy* strips began appearing in newspapers, Cathy Guisewite called me to let me know how much she liked them. But she had not yet seen this one. So I felt compelled to warn her by saying, "Well, just so you know, on Sunday, you become very fat and fly into a bug zapper and are electrocuted."

This was a very popular croc series.

I knew when I drew this series that Alex Trebek no longer had a mustache. But I thought it made him more identifiable. So I drew him with it, knowing full well that readers would later send me e-mails like this one: "Nice job on Alex Trebek. Perhaps you missed the episode where he shaved his mustache?"

After these strips ran, an employee of *Jeopardy* wrote to say that the show's executive producer really loved the series, especially this particular strip. They said they were in the process of renovating the stage and would like to include a print of this strip on the stage wall. I sent it to them and in exchange, Alex Trebek sent me a signed photo. (In which he has no mustache.)

STORY UPDATE:

Larry the Croc has been on "Celebrity Jeopardy." Because of his ability to absorb the "History Channel" while asleep on the couch, he has been more knowledgeable than expected and is winning the game.

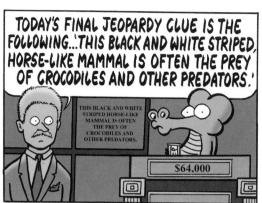

The last strip in a series is often hard to make funny, because you're generally more concerned with wrapping up the storyline than you are with just being funny. But I thought this one came out pretty good.

Panel 1:
HEY, RAT...WANT TO HELP ME DO MY NEW JIGSAW PUZZLE?...I'VE BEEN AT IT ALL DAY.

Panel 2:
DUDE, I'VE GOT BETTER THINGS TO DO THAN WASTE MY TIME ON SOME 1,000 PIECE MONSTROSITY.

OH, I DON'T LIKE THOSE EITHER, SO I BUY THE ONES THAT ARE A LITTLE EASIER.

Panel 3:

Panel 4:
I'M OPEN TO SUGGESTIONS.

Panel 5:
I'M THINKING ABOUT RUNNING FOR THE SENATE...I WANT TO MAKE A DIFFERENCE.

GOOD FOR YOU. WHAT WOULD YOU LIKE TO MAKE A DIFFERENCE IN?

Panel 6:
MY SAVINGS ACCOUNT BY TAKING BRIBES.

Panel 7:
GO AWAY.

PLEASE, SIR. HELP MAKE A DIFFERENCE.

Panel 8:
WOW. THAT GIRL IS PRETTY.

SAY SOMETHING TO HER...DON'T YOU HAVE A DECENT OPENING LINE?

Panel 9:
I HAVEN'T USED AN OPENING LINE ON A GIRL SINCE I WAS AN EIGHTEEN-YEAR-OLD MATH MAJOR IN COLLEGE.

YEAH, WELL, YOU BETTER SAY SOMETHING FAST. SHE'S GETTING UP TO LEAVE.

Panel 10:
DID YOU KNOW THAT PI IS 3.141592653589793238462643383279502884197169399375105820974944592307816406286208 99...?

Panel 11:
WE MATH MAJORS DIDN'T DATE MUCH.

I made extra sure that the Pi number was accurate, as I didn't want to receive two hundred e-mails from snooty math majors around the world.

No hacky sack players wrote in to complain. Apparently, even they don't like hacky sack players.

Well, I avoided the math majors and hacky sack players. But I could not avoid the many people who wrote in to say that bonobos are apes and not monkeys. My only comfort was from a zookeeper who wrote in to say, "I took a poll of the bonobos we have at the San Diego Zoo and most took no offense at the monkey reference."

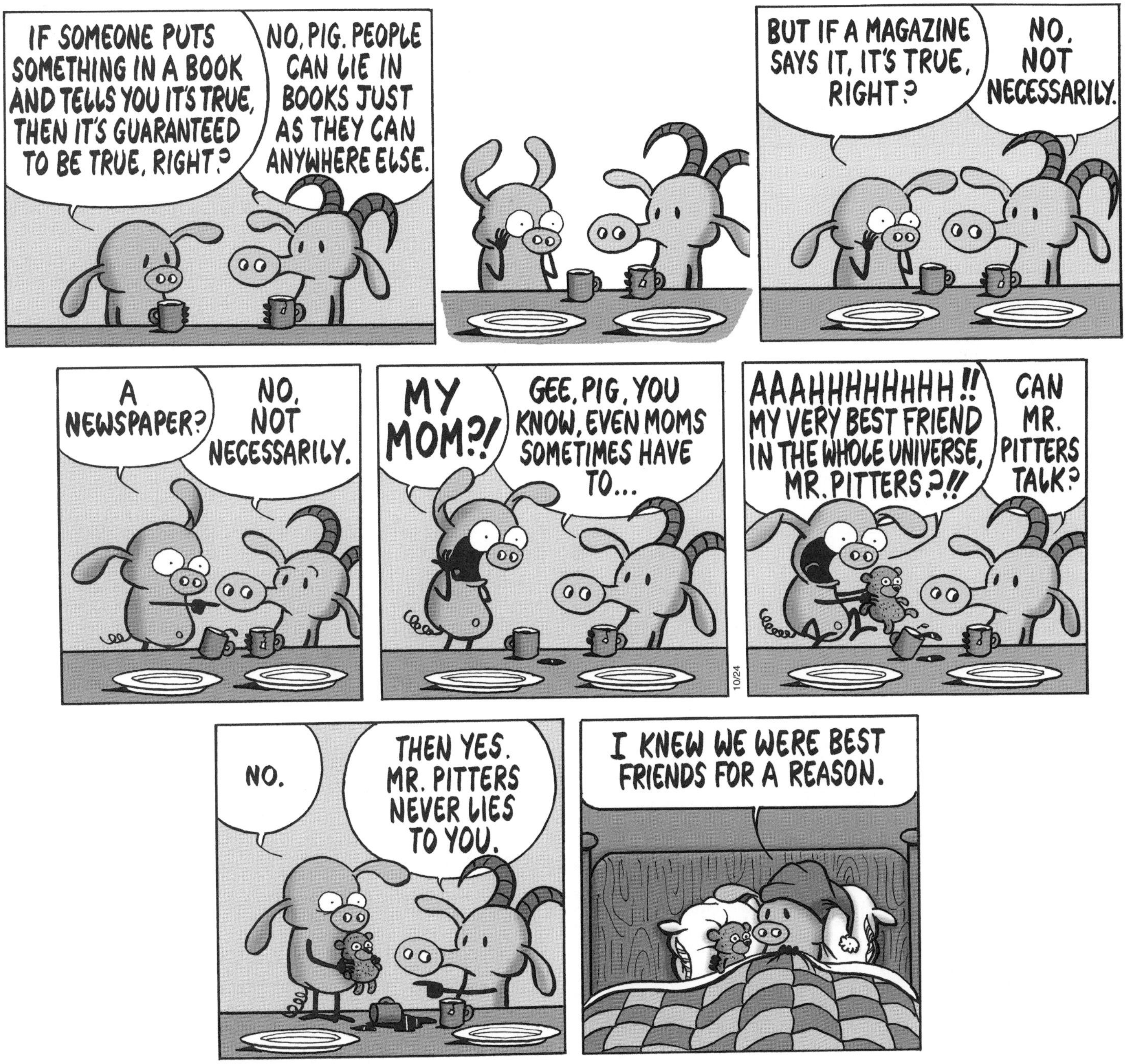
IF SOMEONE PUTS SOMETHING IN A BOOK AND TELLS YOU IT'S TRUE, THEN IT'S GUARANTEED TO BE TRUE, RIGHT?
NO, PIG. PEOPLE CAN LIE IN BOOKS JUST AS THEY CAN ANYWHERE ELSE.
BUT IF A MAGAZINE SAYS IT, IT'S TRUE, RIGHT?
NO. NOT NECESSARILY.
A NEWSPAPER?
NO. NOT NECESSARILY.
MY MOM?!
GEE, PIG, YOU KNOW, EVEN MOMS SOMETIMES HAVE TO...
10/24
AAAHHHHHHHH!! MY VERY BEST FRIEND IN THE WHOLE UNIVERSE, MR. PITTERS?!!
CAN MR. PITTERS TALK?
NO.
THEN YES. MR. PITTERS NEVER LIES TO YOU.
I KNEW WE WERE BEST FRIENDS FOR A REASON.

Pig is very in touch with his feminine side.

We recently bought a house that has an island in the kitchen. Sadly, there are no palm trees.

I like having Pig say things that on the surface are clean enough to run in newspapers, but which simultaneously have an interpretation that is totally inappropriate for newspapers.

Odd that Pig would have a pharaoh costume handy at the diner he goes to. Ah, the miracle of comics.

I was worried that readers wouldn't be able to make out that this guy was a member of the "Biking Baboons," which would ruin the joke. So I wrote it on his helmet, his arm, and his shirt, then drew baboon faces on both his shirt and helmet. I've learned over the years that making the joke dependent on something visually small is very risky because many newspapers shrink their comics tremendously, and some readers just won't be able to make out what you need them to see.

I tried to run this strip close to a national election.

Chez Panisse is a very famous restaurant in Berkeley, California. I was hoping the restaurant would see the strip, be thrilled, and give me a lifetime of free dinners. Didn't happen.

When I wrote this, I thought that Meg Whitman was going to be the next governor of California. But then she lost the election. I ran the strip anyway, figuring that there had to be a woman who became a governor in some state that day.

Mentioning any ethnicity in even a slightly derogatory way is guaranteed to anger a certain segment of the population. So I ran this on a Saturday, when fewer people read the comics.

You know you had to reach a long way for a pun when you have a little dog with a saw jumping on a Kurdish man's head.

199

This is another case of getting away with something that is clean enough to run in newspapers but simultaneously open to edgier interpretation. Because to me, Pig is saying, "You just made me sh#t my pants."

Same here. But this time, Pig's line is so potentially dirty I can't even write it in this treasury.

After reading this, one reader wrote, "I am now envisioning a duel between George Washington and Andy Obelisk."

Hey, that stuff on the ground almost looks like water. I just get better and better.

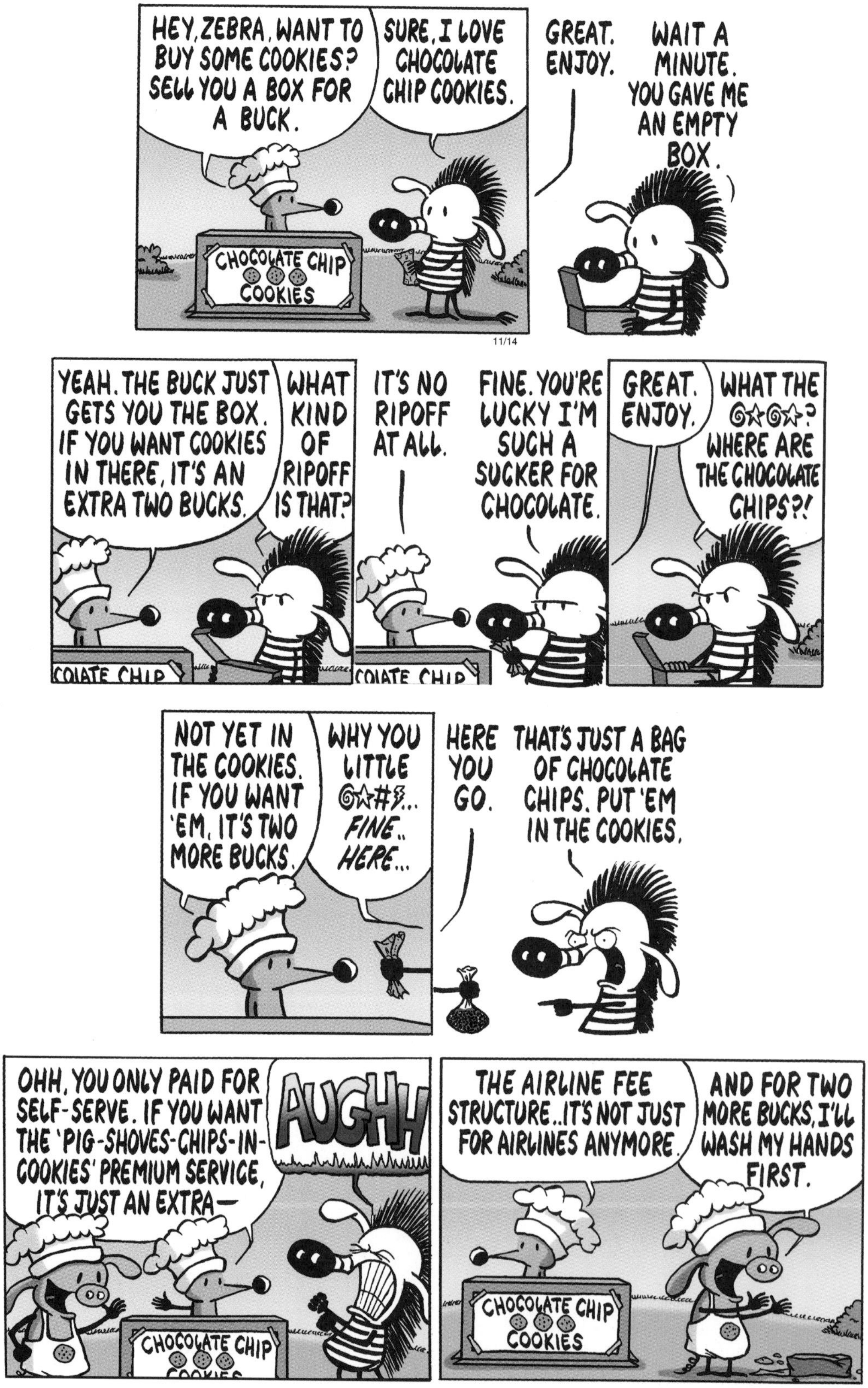
HEY, ZEBRA, WANT TO BUY SOME COOKIES? SELL YOU A BOX FOR A BUCK.
SURE, I LOVE CHOCOLATE CHIP COOKIES.
CHOCOLATE CHIP COOKIES
GREAT. ENJOY.
WAIT A MINUTE. YOU GAVE ME AN EMPTY BOX.
11/14
YEAH. THE BUCK JUST GETS YOU THE BOX. IF YOU WANT COOKIES IN THERE, IT'S AN EXTRA TWO BUCKS.
WHAT KIND OF RIPOFF IS THAT?
IT'S NO RIPOFF AT ALL.
FINE. YOU'RE LUCKY I'M SUCH A SUCKER FOR CHOCOLATE.
GREAT. ENJOY.
WHAT THE @☆@☆? WHERE ARE THE CHOCOLATE CHIPS?!
NOT YET IN THE COOKIES. IF YOU WANT 'EM, IT'S TWO MORE BUCKS.
WHY YOU LITTLE @☆#... FINE.. HERE...
HERE YOU GO.
THAT'S JUST A BAG OF CHOCOLATE CHIPS. PUT 'EM IN THE COOKIES.
OHH, YOU ONLY PAID FOR SELF-SERVE. IF YOU WANT THE 'PIG-SHOVES-CHIPS-IN-COOKIES' PREMIUM SERVICE, IT'S JUST AN EXTRA—
AUGHH
CHOCOLATE CHIP
THE AIRLINE FEE STRUCTURE..IT'S NOT JUST FOR AIRLINES ANYMORE.
AND FOR TWO MORE BUCKS, I'LL WASH MY HANDS FIRST.
CHOCOLATE CHIP COOKIES

I can't believe it took me nine years of doing *Pearls* to make my first dung beetle joke. I'm sort of ashamed.

I made Rat's speech balloon in the first panel bigger than usual to cover up the other "ZZZZZZZ" on the wall behind them.

Admission time: I may or may not go on Wikipedia from time to time to alter the biography of another syndicated cartoonist. This may have included changing his influences from "Charles Schulz, *MAD* magazine, and Gary Larson" to "Stephan Pastis only . . . he is like a god to me."

I really like *Cul de Sac*. I try to promote it as often as I can.

This triggered a flood of questions as to what the pun was going to be. It was going to be some play on the quote, "Don't shoot until you see the whites of their eyes."

As a kid, I used to do this all the time with the Sunday comics. The Silly Putty would pick up the image and you could then stretch the Silly Putty to distort the look of the character. I'm told that with the type of newsprint now used, you can no longer do this.

Clearly, Rat and Pig haven't looked at their own arms and legs.

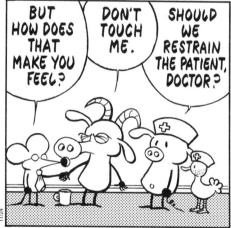

The quote on the window is based on an old campaign for Mounds and Almond Joy candy bars. But it probably went over the heads of anyone under twenty years old.

I don't know why, but this one really made me laugh.

WHAT ARE YOU LOOKING AT?

MY COUSIN SENT A MASS E-MAIL TO ME AND ALL OUR RELATIVES INVITING US TO HIS ENGAGEMENT PARTY.

11/28

THE FUNNY PART IS THAT OTHER THAN ME, HE CAN'T STAND ANY OF OUR RELATIVES... HE'S JUST INVITING THEM BECAUSE HE FEELS HE HAS TO. LOOK AT THE REPLY I'M SENDING...

I'll be there, cousin...And with any luck, the rest of the dimwitted blowhards we call our "relatives" won't be...(And a good time can be had by all!)

THAT'S GREAT.

THANKS.

⚡SEND⚡

MY FAVORITE PART WAS HOW YOU DIDN'T CLICK 'REPLY.' YOU CLICKED 'REPLY ALL.'

AHHHHHHHHHHHHHHHH

'REPLY ALL'...THE DEADLIEST CLICK IN COMPUTERDOM.

UNCLE TOM?...HEY...LISTEN... DON'T PICK UP E-MAIL FOR THE REST OF YOUR LIFE...

I think this is the first time I've drawn Goat with his antlers straightened out. He looks a bit unicorn-esque. The popping eyeballs are something I once saw in *Calvin and Hobbes*.

This series was supposed to be loosely based on the *Deepwater Horizon* oil spill from the summer of 2010.

This seemed like a good idea until I had to draw all those gophers. Then I began to hate my own brain.

Chemical dispersants were one of the methods they used to try and break up the *Deepwater Horizon* oil before it reached the shore.

By about this time in the week, I was wishing I had an assistant to whom I could have said, "Dude, go draw a ton of &%$#$#% gophers."

By this point in the week, my hand refused to draw any more gophers. So I just copied and pasted these guys from the 11/30 strip (the one that shows the oil derrick exploding).

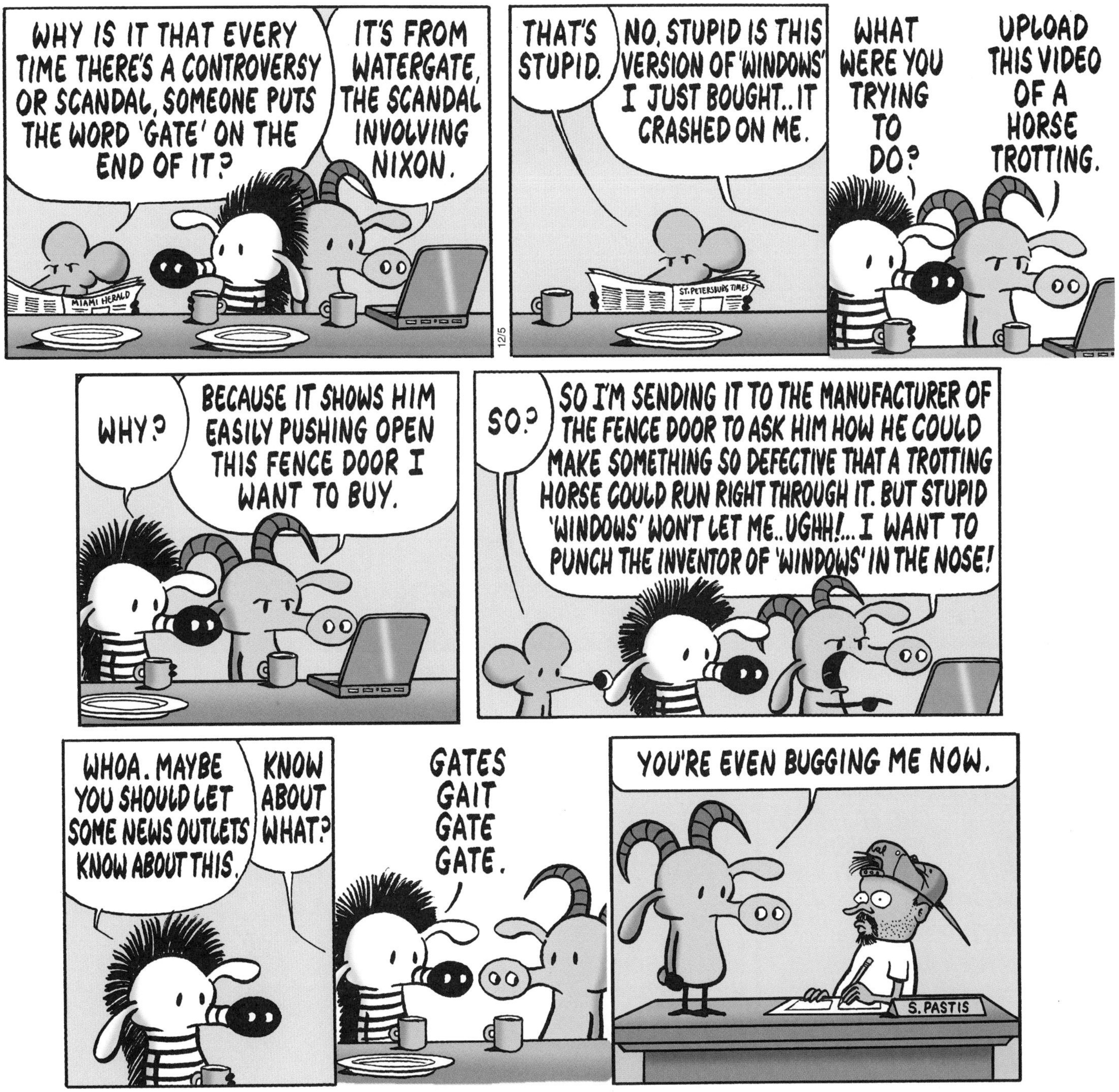

WHY IS IT THAT EVERY TIME THERE'S A CONTROVERSY OR SCANDAL, SOMEONE PUTS THE WORD 'GATE' ON THE END OF IT?
IT'S FROM WATERGATE, THE SCANDAL INVOLVING NIXON.
MIAMI HERALD
12/5
THAT'S STUPID.
NO, STUPID IS THIS VERSION OF 'WINDOWS' I JUST BOUGHT.. IT CRASHED ON ME.
ST. PETERSBURG TIMES
WHAT WERE YOU TRYING TO DO?
UPLOAD THIS VIDEO OF A HORSE TROTTING.
WHY?
BECAUSE IT SHOWS HIM EASILY PUSHING OPEN THIS FENCE DOOR I WANT TO BUY.
SO?
SO I'M SENDING IT TO THE MANUFACTURER OF THE FENCE DOOR TO ASK HIM HOW HE COULD MAKE SOMETHING SO DEFECTIVE THAT A TROTTING HORSE COULD RUN RIGHT THROUGH IT. BUT STUPID 'WINDOWS' WON'T LET ME.. UGHH!... I WANT TO PUNCH THE INVENTOR OF 'WINDOWS' IN THE NOSE!
WHOA. MAYBE YOU SHOULD LET SOME NEWS OUTLETS KNOW ABOUT THIS.
KNOW ABOUT WHAT?
GATES GAIT GATE GATE.
YOU'RE EVEN BUGGING ME NOW.
S. PASTIS

AHHHH! More gophers! Thank goodness for anvils.

My son plays this game all the time with me. He always spots the Volkswagen before I do and punches me. So after awhile, I just start punching him for any car I see.

My wife, Staci, had these shades installed in our house. I think she did it to prevent me from accidentally getting myself tied up in the cord.

"Bread goes in. Toast comes out." This should be the entire instructional manual for a toaster.

Men seem to compare flat screen TV sizes the way they once compared car engines.

This was inspired by a Thomas Jefferson quote: "I tremble for my country when I reflect that God is just."

For those who might not know, the characters in panel 3 are from the comic strip *Doonesbury* by Garry Trudeau. In 2009 and 2010, I went to Iraq and Afghanistan with Garry on USO trips to visit the soldiers. During the Afghanistan trip, Garry did a drawing of Uncle Duke for me in which Uncle Duke is saying, "Who the $&#$ is Stephan?"

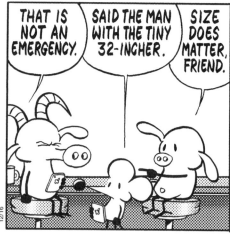

For the record, I think my own TV is a measly 46". So Rat would probably be sending me the same e-mails.

The beginning of a heartwarming *Pearls* Christmas tale.

I see so many people using the comics as wrapping paper, I figured I'd make it easy for them.

For reasons I can't explain, Santa's feet are each turned 90 degrees to the right. Perhaps Larry broke his ankles.

I like Larry best when he thinks he's fooling somebody.

Santa's ankles aren't quite as broken here.

Most cartoonists draw Christmas strips where all the characters are together in a cozy house filled with presents. I have an elf get his leg chewed off.

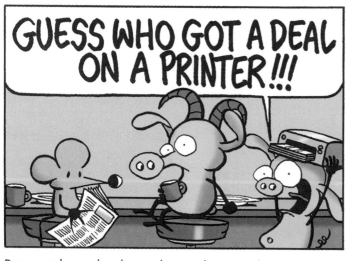

Rat must keep that bat in his pocket. It's always around when he needs it.

This strip and the next one are really old strips that for one reason or another, I never got around to running.

This was a very popular strip, as are most of the pun ones.

I drew this hairy-looking guy on the wall of the room where I write, and I liked the way he looked. So I created a strip for him to appear in.

I drew this strip and the next one after I returned from my USO trip to Iraq. We used Black Hawk helicopters to get from base to base.

Unbelievably enough, this is how I am when I watch certain games. If the team I'm rooting for is doing well, I won't move anything in the room, thinking that somehow the placement of these items matters. And yes, I'm that broken in the head.

I recently went to New Orleans and had my first bowl of gumbo. Fortunately, there were no green arms in it.

I wrote this after Wikileaks began releasing thousands of government documents to the public. I do not believe my diary was included.

HEYA, RHONDA ROBIN. WHAT'S GOING ON?

JUST FINISHED RAISING MY CHICK. ALL THAT'S LEFT IS TO GET HIM OUT OF THE NEST AND HAVE HIM START LIVING HIS OWN LIFE.

PUSH

THUD

SOMETIMES YOU HAVE TO HELP.

If you're wondering why I kept the bird on his head in the third panel, that makes two of us. I should have drawn him lying on his side. If you want, cut him out of the book, turn him sideways, and tape the book back together.

HAD TO CALL THE STUPID CABLE COMPANY. I'LL TELL YOU, NO MATTER WHERE I LOOK THESE DAYS, I CAN'T FIND ONE COMPANY THAT GIVES GOOD SERVICE.

AH, YES. REMINDS ME OF THIS BOOK I'M READING ON THE ANCIENT GREEK PHILOSOPHER DIOGENES. HE CARRIED A LANTERN THROUGH ALL OF GREECE SEARCHING FOR JUST ONE HONEST MAN.

EEERT EEERT EEERT

YOU SET OFF MY BORING GUY-OMETER.

WHY DO I TRY?

PSST.. AVOID THE WORDS 'ANCIENT,' 'BOOK,' AND 'READING.'

Growing up, I learned so many things about famous people or events simply because I'd seen them mentioned in a *Peanuts* comic strip or a Bugs Bunny cartoon. Whether it's a Wagnerian opera or *War and Peace*, odds are my first exposure to it came from one of these sources. So now that I'm a syndicated cartoonist, I try to include stuff like this reference to Diogenes, knowing that some little kid will read it and one day know who that person was because of it.

WHAT ARE YOU DOING, RAT?

I AM DIOGERAT. I WALK THE WORLD WITH MY LANTERN LOOKING FOR JUST ONE COMPANY THAT GIVES GOOD SERVICE.

WHAT HAVE YOU FOUND?

THAT I'D HAVE BETTER LUCK FINDING ELVIS.

I THINK HE'S DEAD.

THANKS, MORON. I KNOW.

CHECK, PLEASE.

I wrote this after getting off the phone with a very frustrating service representative from my cable company. Little did she know how much her idiocy inspired me.

I know too many people like this.

Hey, I got away with saying the word "crappy." Score one for the good guys.

FADE IN:

JEFFY, fat and tattooed, sits on death row receiving last rites.

JEFFY
Skip it, Reverend. The Jeffy don't fear death.

Having been to two war zones with the real-life "Jeffy" Keane, I can tell you that he does, in fact, fear death. At the first sign of danger, he'd cry and run off, leaving a dotted line behind him.

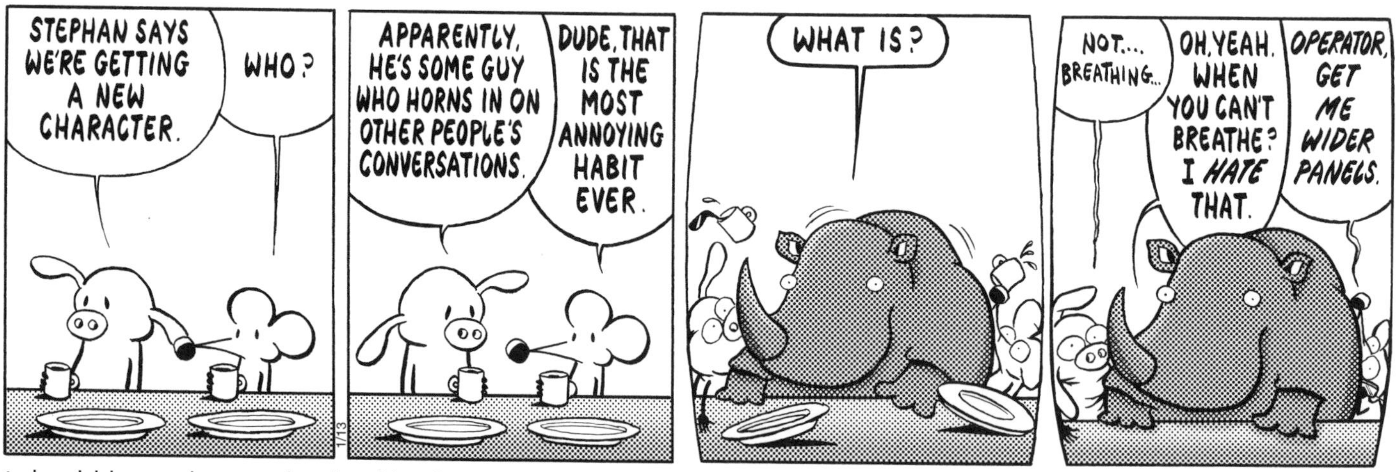
STEPHAN SAYS WE'RE GETTING A NEW CHARACTER.
WHO?
APPARENTLY, HE'S SOME GUY WHO HORNS IN ON OTHER PEOPLE'S CONVERSATIONS.
DUDE, THAT IS THE MOST ANNOYING HABIT EVER.
WHAT IS?
NOT... BREATHING...
OH, YEAH. WHEN YOU CAN'T BREATHE? I *HATE* THAT.
OPERATOR, GET ME WIDER PANELS.
1/13

I should bring this guy back. I like the way he looks.

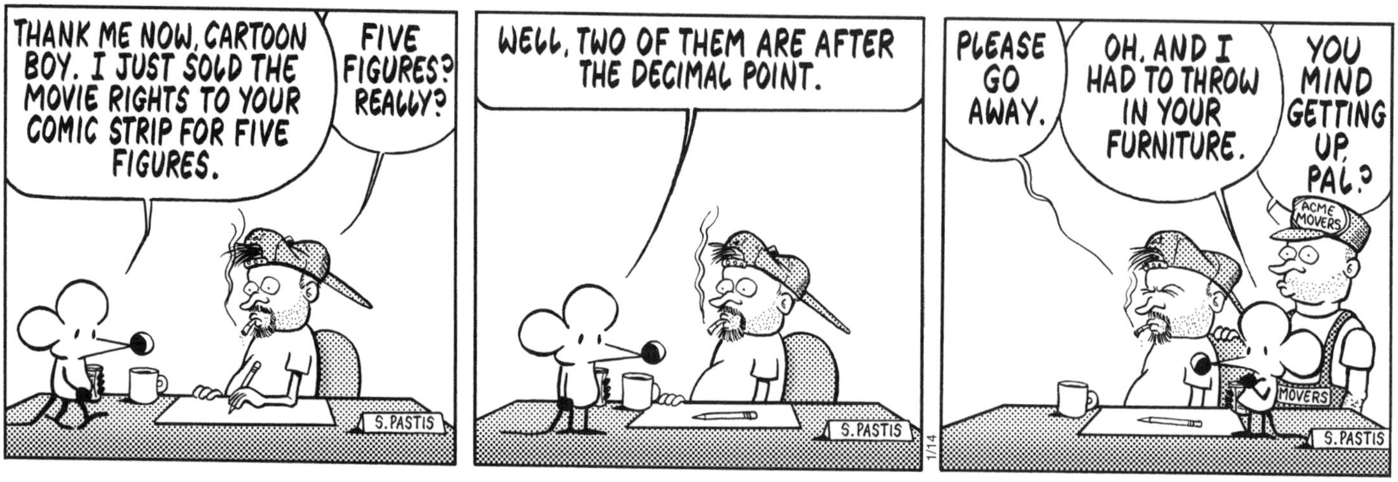
THANK ME NOW, CARTOON BOY. I JUST SOLD THE MOVIE RIGHTS TO YOUR COMIC STRIP FOR FIVE FIGURES.
FIVE FIGURES? REALLY?
S. PASTIS
WELL, TWO OF THEM ARE AFTER THE DECIMAL POINT.
S. PASTIS
1/14
PLEASE GO AWAY.
OH, AND I HAD TO THROW IN YOUR FURNITURE.
YOU MIND GETTING UP, PAL?
ACME MOVERS
MOVERS
S. PASTIS

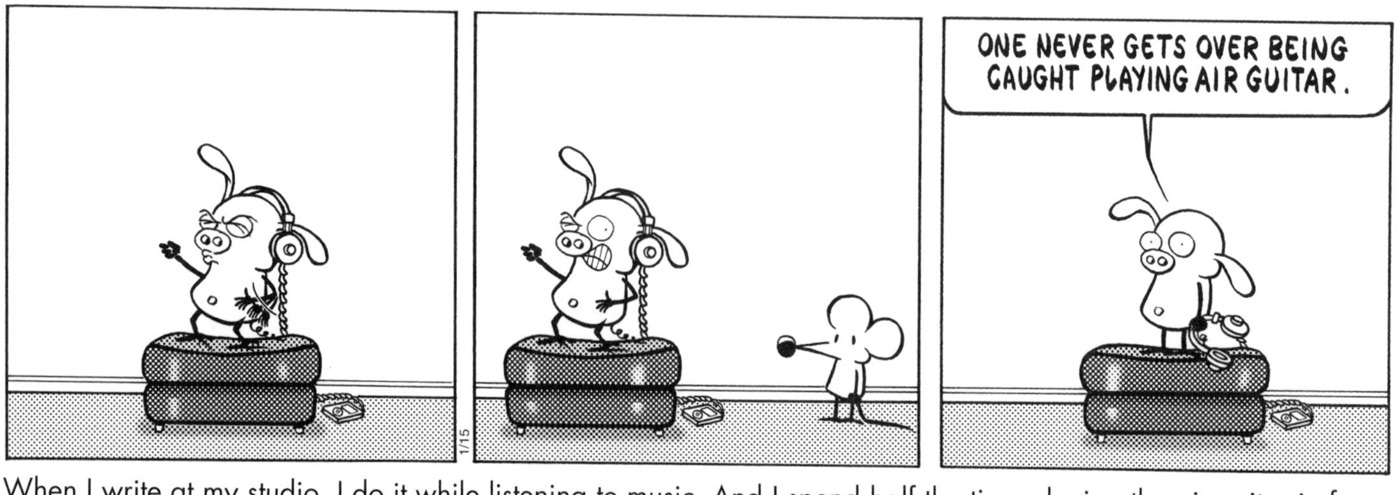
1/15
ONE NEVER GETS OVER BEING CAUGHT PLAYING AIR GUITAR.

When I write at my studio, I do it while listening to music. And I spend half the time playing the air guitar in front of the mirror. Don't laugh. I look really cool doing it. Okay . . . *I* think I look really cool doing it.

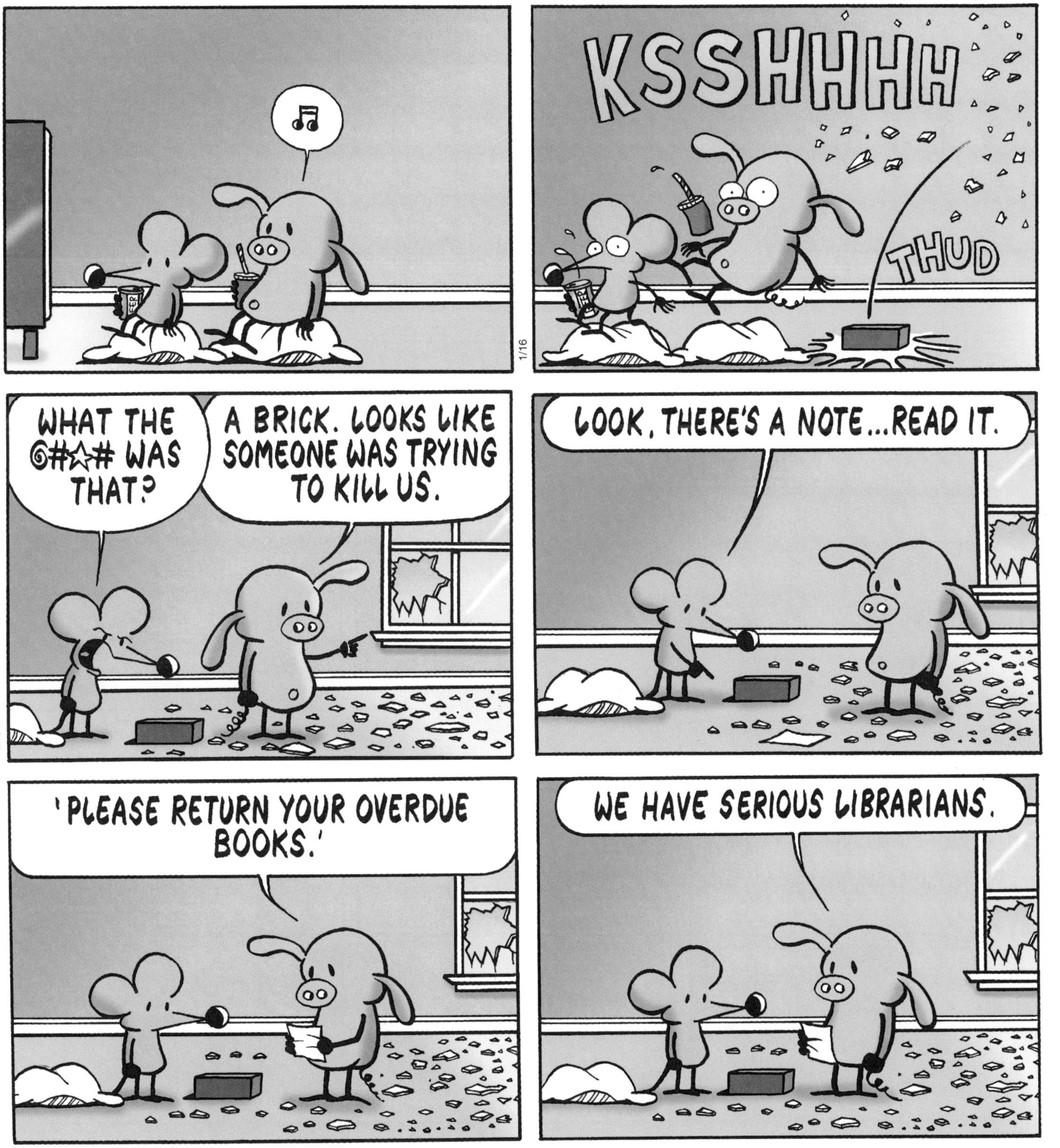
KSSHHHH
THUD
1/16
WHAT THE @#☆# WAS THAT?
A BRICK. LOOKS LIKE SOMEONE WAS TRYING TO KILL US.
LOOK, THERE'S A NOTE...READ IT.
'PLEASE RETURN YOUR OVERDUE BOOKS.'
WE HAVE SERIOUS LIBRARIANS.

I recently learned through someone at my syndicate that Bill Watterson has apparently watched some of the videos I've made to promote the *Pearls* books. Just learning that he knows who I am was unbelievably exciting.

That is one well-drawn tire. I wonder if Bill Watterson noticed that.

230

That is one well-drawn rake. I wonder if Bill Watterson noticed that.

I picked on Des Moines here because *Pearls* does not run in the newspaper there. That's the price a city must pay for not running my strip.

Unfortunately, I have to turn down most friend requests I get on Facebook because Facebook limits you to five thousand friends. So I started what's called a "Fan Page." To find it, just search for "Stephan Pastis Author" on Facebook.

This strip and the next one are very old strips that I just never ran. I'm not sure why. I like both of them.

Crocs named "Bob" do not fare well. I think dozens of them have died.

WHAT ARE YOU DOING? / **EDITING THE DICTIONARY. I'M CROSSING OUT WORDS WE DON'T NEED ANYMORE AND REPLACING THEM WITH ONES WE DO. THE FIRST TO GET THE AXE WAS 'FORTNIGHT.'**

WHAT'S WRONG WITH 'FORTNIGHT'? / **UNNECESSARY. NORMAL PEOPLE SAY 'TWO WEEKS.' IT'S ONLY PURPOSE IS TO MAKE POMPOUS PEOPLE FEEL POMPOUSER.**

SINCE WHEN IS 'POMPOUSER' A WORD? / **SINCE IT REPLACED 'FORTNIGHT.'**

YOU ARE NOT REPLACING 'FORTNIGHT.' / **WHOA. YOU'RE SOUNDING POMPOUSER AND POMPOUSER.**

Do you know anyone who uses the word "fortnight"?

HEY, LOOK, PIG...IT'S THAT GUY YOU SEE ON THOSE T.V. COMMERCIALS...THE ONE YOU POKE IN THE BELLY AND HE GIGGLES. / **HEY, YOU'RE RIGHT... I'LL TRY IT.**

POKE POKE

GUESS HE'S DIFFERENT IN PERSON.

This was a really popular strip. Even better, I wasn't sued.

BOING BOING BOING BOING

OUR RENT IS DUE. WE HAVE NO CASH. I LOST IT AT THE TRACK. WE'RE BEING EVICTED.

BOING BOING BOING BOING

BAD NEWS IS BEST DELIVERED ON A POGO STICK.

This strip was a mess. I must have changed Rat's lines in the second panel more than twenty times. I probably should have given up at some point, but I had gone to all the trouble of drawing it and didn't want to lose the strip.

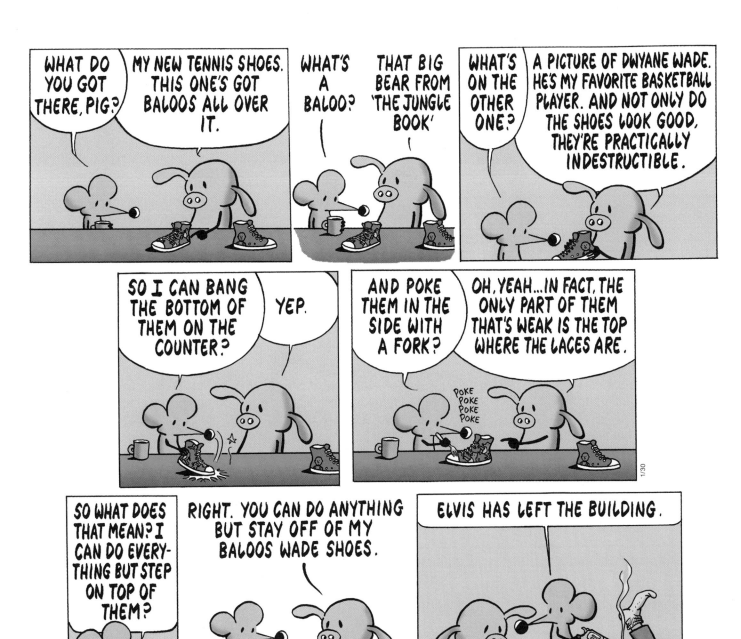

You could win a lot of bar bets asking people how Dwyane Wade spells his first name. Looks odd every time I see it.

My dad owned a pickup truck and this sort of thing always happened to him. I think he sort of resented it.

In case you were wondering, President Obama did not call and ask for the original of this strip.

This is not a good strip. Something about the rhythm is really off. Please continue on as though it never happened.

Seeing the phrase "iambic pentameter" suddenly reminds me why I hated high school English.

I wonder if the newspaper editors whose job it is to review the comics page actually took the time to read all the writing in the third panel.

This is another strip that started out as a sketch. I drew Rat as you see him there in the third panel and liked how he looked so much that I just built a strip around it. Often when that happens, I won't even re-draw the image. I'll just scan it in straight from my sketchbook.

The way you know that's bread Rat is holding is that it says "BREAD" on it.

240

The ninth image of Pig (the one just before the final panel) is supposed to be the Elaine dance from *Seinfeld*.

Pig swearing (sort of). I think this and the British Petroleum strip (7/15/10) are the only two times that's happened.

Ah, the perils of having to write the strip in advance. I wrote this strip immediately after the Arab Spring began in Tunisia in January 2011. But by the time it ran six weeks later, the revolution in Egypt had begun and the story had moved on. This is the one real regret I have with doing a syndicated comic. About the soonest I can get a strip to run is approximately four to six weeks after the date I draw it.

Aunt Vivian is my mom's sister. I called her in advance to say, "Hey, I just wanted to let you know you're in the strip." She said, "Well, that's nice." I then said, "You're a dead ham."

And yes, Uncle George is my Aunt Vivian's husband.

243

Clive was named for the real-life owner of Calistoga Roastery, a cafe in Calistoga, California, where I often write the strip. The original of this strip hangs on the wall.

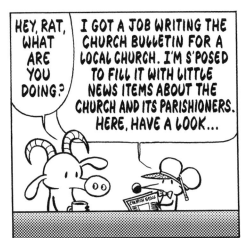

After this ran, a former church bulletin editor wrote to me to say, "I have to admit . . . stories like that would get more people reading the bulletin instead of the usual announcements about bake sales and spaghetti dinners." And a retired priest wrote to me to say thanks on behalf of "millions of other ministers."

This was a very popular strip. So $#%&# you, Rat.

I'm tempted to make Scientist Bob a regular character.

What better way to go out than with a threat to "knock a few heads." See you in the next treasury.

The Drawings You Probably Never Saw

The Sunday comics page is an odd animal. Mostly because the amount of space and the number of comics a newspaper has can vary so widely.

So you see all sorts of different things. Some newspapers run your strip large. Some run it small. Some run it horizontal. Some run it vertical.

In the best-case scenario (or worst, depending on your art skills), the newspaper gives you a whole bunch of room, including space for a title panel.

While such roomy newspapers are now the exception (especially in this age of the incredibly shrinking newspaper), they still do exist in some places.

Thus, as a cartoonist, you are required to always submit a title panel. Despite the fact that most people won't see it.

In the beginning, I changed my title panel frequently. I was a very ambitious young lad.

Now I am old and fat, and use the same one every week.

But I realize now that most people probably never saw those early title panels.

Thus, I provide them here, in all their glory and shame.

This was the very first title panel. It's very bad. So don't look.

This was one I used a couple years later. It's better than the first one. But still not great.

Here I'm starting to get quite artsy-fartsy.

Around this time I started doing parodies of famous rock albums. This one was of the Janis Joplin album, *Pearl*. Given the title of my strip, I thought it was an obvious choice.

This was a parody of U2's album, *The Joshua Tree*. I almost made this a book cover, but then I saw that Berkeley Breathed had already done such an image with his *Bloom County* characters, so I decided against it.

Pearls Before Swine, 2004
Pen on paper, 4" x 8"
Stephan Pastis Collection

This one did become a book cover. I used a re-drawn version of it for the
cover of the *Pearls* collection, *Nighthogs*.